THE UK AIR FRYER COOKBOOK

Many easy, quick, and delicious recipes for every day.
Including tips and tricks for beginners

Olivia K. Foster

© Copyright 2023 by [Olivia K. Foster]

All rights reserved. No part of this guide may be reproduced in any form without permission in writing from the publisher except in the case of brief quotation embodied in critical articles or reviews.

INTRODUCTION	4
HOW DOES AN AIR FRYER WORK?	4
IMPORTANT FACTORS TO CONSIDER WHEN PURCHASING AN AIR FRYER:	5
BENEFITS OF OWNING AN AIR FRYER	7
CLEANING TIPS FOR YOUR AIR FRYER	9
HOW TO DEEP CLEAN AN AIR FRYER	9
BREAKFAST	11
BEEF, PORK, AND LAMB	21
POULTRY RECIPES	32
FISH & SEAFOOD RECIPES	43
VEGETARIAN RECIPES	51
SNACKS AND APPETIZERS	59
DESSERTS	68

INTRODUCTION

What exactly is an air fryer? An air fryer is known as a fryer without oil. This name alone reveals the journey's destination.

However, because an air fryer performs differently than a traditional fryer, you should not add oil or grease to it.

Healthy air fryer for roasting, roasting, baking, and grating. All of these preparations are possible with the air fryer. The most famous specialty is preparing low-fat French fries, croquettes, and chicken nuggets. For example, a kilogram of fresh potato stalks and a tablespoon of oil can be used to make crisp French fries.

Furthermore, all pre-fried frozen dishes can be wonderfully crispy roasted without fat if time is of the essence. A crisp outcome may be obtained rapidly thanks to a unique combination of hot air that circulates swiftly and precisely and the right temperature in a compact cooking area. Rather than being immersed in boiling oil, as in a standard deep fryer, the food is showered in hot air.

The air fryer does not need to be warmed up; simply set the temperature and timer, and you're good to go! You no longer must worry about storing or disposing of cooking oil. The closed cooking chamber allows less odor and unpleasant oil droplets on the skin or work area.

This air fryer can cook much more than fish sticks and french fries. You can bake a superb cake or a typical potato or vegetable gratin in the proper cake or gratin dish. You will receive a free copy of the recipe book "Crispy Baked" as inspiration, giving you a taste of the range of possible recipes.

HOW DOES AN AIR FRYER WORK?

The look of an air fryer may differ depending on the brand, size, and price. However, there are a few components to be aware of, namely:
- a heating element
- a fan
- a drawer where the food is placed
- the controls, which are normally located on the front of the air fryer
- a basket or grating those lifts and retains the food contained within the drawer

You can better understand how the air fryer works if you are aware of these components.

The cooking processes

To begin, it is essential to understand that an air fryer does not properly cook your food. When food is fried, it is cooked in hot oil. Although frying involves the use of oil, you may shallow fry in a pan or deep fry in a skillet with the oil around the food.

In theory, an air fryer is like a deep fryer in that the heat source completely envelops the food and touches its whole surface area at once (in the case of deep frying, hot oil). Deep frying provides quickly crispy food since the item absorbs strong heat all at once.

The air fryer, like a convection oven, cooks food. After setting the temperature, you place the meal in the cooking drawer. The fan circulates the hot air produced by the heating element swiftly.

IMPORTANT FACTORS TO CONSIDER WHEN PURCHASING AN AIR FRYER:

- What kind of air fryer do you want?
- What size do you require?
- How would you want to clean it?
- What is your financial situation?

What kind of air fryer do you want?

Classic air fryers

These days, classic air fryers are the most popular. They come with a removable air fryer basket and can be cleaned in the dishwasher in most cases.
Some are egg-shaped, while others are square, with square-shaped ones becoming increasingly common. The square-shaped ones have the advantage of providing greater room for cooking meals in a single layer.
Who is it useful for? Anyone! Most folks will be satisfied with a traditional air fryer.

Air fryer oven

An air fryer oven, often known as an air fryer toaster oven, resembles a miniature oven. The difference between it and a standard convection oven is that it is smaller, so it heats up faster, and it comes with a mesh air fryer basket or tray. This means you receive the same circulating hot air advantage as a square air fryer.
An air fryer oven can hold more food, especially when cooking in a single layer, but it also takes up more area. Food will take somewhat longer to cook in an air fryer oven than in a traditional air fryer, but it will cook faster than in a standard oven.

Air fryer lids

An air fryer lid is a lid that you may use to convert an instant pot or other pressure cooker into an air fryer. Aside from an air fryer lid, you'll need an air fryer basket that's compatible with your pressure cooker.

What size do you require?

Air fryers come in varying sizes, from super small to quite large. What size you should choose depends on how many people you wish to cook for at once.
A smaller air fryer will heat up faster and cook your food faster, whilst a larger one will allow you to cook more at once.

What is your financial situation?

Another key factor to consider is your financial situation. Air fryers can range in price from $30 to several hundred dollars. As predicted, finding a tiny air fryer * for a lesser price is easy.

How would you want to clean it?

Most air fryers contain dishwasher-safe parts, but if this is essential to you, be sure it is true for the type you are considering.

BENEFITS OF OWNING AN AIR FRYER

Healthier Cooking

The idea of healthier cooking is the single most important consideration for most individuals purchasing an air fryer. With very little oil needed in the cooking process, this is an excellent method to substitute unhealthy deep-fried items with a healthier option.
You still need to spray fried dishes with oil, such as breaded chicken tenders and fried fish, so the breading gets equally crispy when cooking, but the amount of oil you need is significantly less. You may also prepare French fries and tater tots without deep-frying to obtain a great crispy outcome.

Quick, safe, and simple to use

The air fryer began as a kind of substitute for a deep fryer. While it was fantastic, it wasn't enough to persuade most people that they needed one, because few people use a deep fryer daily at home.
A typical issue these days is that we all want to cook more regularly but just don't have the time. Therefore, pre-packaged meals and take out are so popular, despite the fact that we all know how terrible they are. Wouldn't you rather prepare items like salmon or pork chops in the air fryer in under 20 minutes than order out?
Cooking at home becomes a lot more enticing option because air fryers are quick and easy to use Dinner is simplified thanks to the air fryer. Simply season a piece of meat, such as a chicken breast (even from frozen), place it in the basket, and set it to cook. So straightforward.

Food that is crisp and crunchy

This is the best reason if you prepare a lot of frozen and breaded items like onion rings and chicken tenders. Instead of a soggy mess, the air fryer crisps up the food you cook, resulting in a crispy and golden surface.
All you need is a little spray cooking oil on the outside of the meal to get a crisp and crispy exterior. This is the ideal method for making anything breaded, as well as any frozen or breaded dish.
Consider reheating leftover pizza! It not only crisps the bottom crust but also revitalizes the toppings as it warms the slice through. When it's finished, it'll be just as good as the first day.

It's Extremely Versatile

The air fryer is much more than just a healthier alternative to deep-frying. In reality, this gadget can prepare almost everything, from fried chicken to entire spaghetti squash to curries and sweets.
Yes, it's ideal for reheating frozen store-bought dishes such as French fries, tater tots, and pizza rolls. It's so simple that even children can do it. That takes care of dinner.

Cooking in the air fryer is faster than cooking in the oven.

An air fryer has the benefit of becoming extremely hot very quickly, and the circulating air helps the food cook evenly, being browned and crispy without any assistance from you. This implies you'll be able to reduce the amount of time you spend cooking.

An air fryer cooks faster than an oven, not only because it heats up rapidly, but also because it is smaller than an oven. An oven normally requires up to 10 minutes to pre-heat, but the air fryer requires no pre-heating time for most recipes.

This means you can load your meal into the basket, slip it into the air fryer, set the timer, and enjoy in 10-15 minutes.

It's ideal for quick and simple snacking. It's very simple to switch it on, throw in your favourite food, and cook it to perfection in minutes, whether for a party or an after-school treat.

Reheat Foods Easily

Not only can you cook most foods in an air fryer, but you can also reheat meals in it, making it even more versatile. There are a few reasons why you would wish to reheat food in an air fryer.

- It's a quick and simple method of reheating food.
- It prevents food from burning or overcooking.
- It's simple.
- It keeps the meal crisp and flavourful.

Simple to Clean

Is there anyone on the planet who doesn't despise cleaning up after a meal? The fact is that this tedious activity may sap much of the enjoyment from a delicious dinner. As a result, you'll be pleased to learn that a decent air fryer is also quite simple to clean after use.

If you keep up with cleaning it after each use, it will just need a routine clean, just like any other pot or pan you use. Simply fill the basket with soapy water and scrub the interior and outside with a non-scratch sponge. Some air fryer baskets are also dishwasher safe.

You should also undertake a thorough cleaning of the entire device, including the cooking coil, once or twice a month, depending on how frequently you use it. Cleaning the oven is not a difficult or time-consuming task if done on a regular basis.

CLEANING TIPS FOR YOUR AIR FRYER

Before you deep clean your air fryer, familiarize yourself with the maintenance dos and don'ts.
- Steel wire brushes, abrasive sponges, or metal tools should not be used to clean the residue and food particles from your air fryer. This may have an impact on the non-stick coating on the stove surface.
- Keep your air fryer away from water. Because it is an electric appliance, the main unit will be affected.
- While cleaning, make sure your fryer is turned off.
- If you notice a bad odour emanating from your air fryer, try scraping stuck-on food from the crevices using a wooden skewer, toothpick, or even an old toothbrush. These buried crumbs might eventually ignite, emitting a foul odour and burning the machine.
- To assist with residual odours, massage the cooking surface and basket with a half-lemon split in half. Allow for at least 30 minutes before cleaning.
- Use cleaning solutions that are safe to consume. Disinfectants that have not been approved for use around food should not be utilized.

HOW TO DEEP CLEAN AN AIR FRYER

1. Begin by disconnecting your air fryer if you have recently used it. Allow it to cool for 30 minutes.
2. Remove the baskets and pans from the dishwasher and wash them in hot, soapy water. Allow at least 10 minutes for each of these sections to soak in hot, soapy water before washing them clean with a non-abrasive sponge if any have food or oil baked on them. If you wish to clean them in the dishwasher, check your instructions to determine if they are dishwasher safe.
3. To clean the interior, use a moist microfiber cloth or a non-abrasive sponge soaked in dish soap. Using a clean, wet cloth, remove the soap.
4. While the device is upside down, wipe the heating element with a damp cloth or sponge.
5. Make a paste of water and baking soda if the primary appliance has any baked-on or hard residue. With a soft-bristled scrub brush, work the paste into the residue before wiping it away with a clean towel.
6. Clean the exterior using a damp cloth. Using a clean, moist towel, remove the soap.
7. Before reassembling, dry the main unit and any detachable pieces.

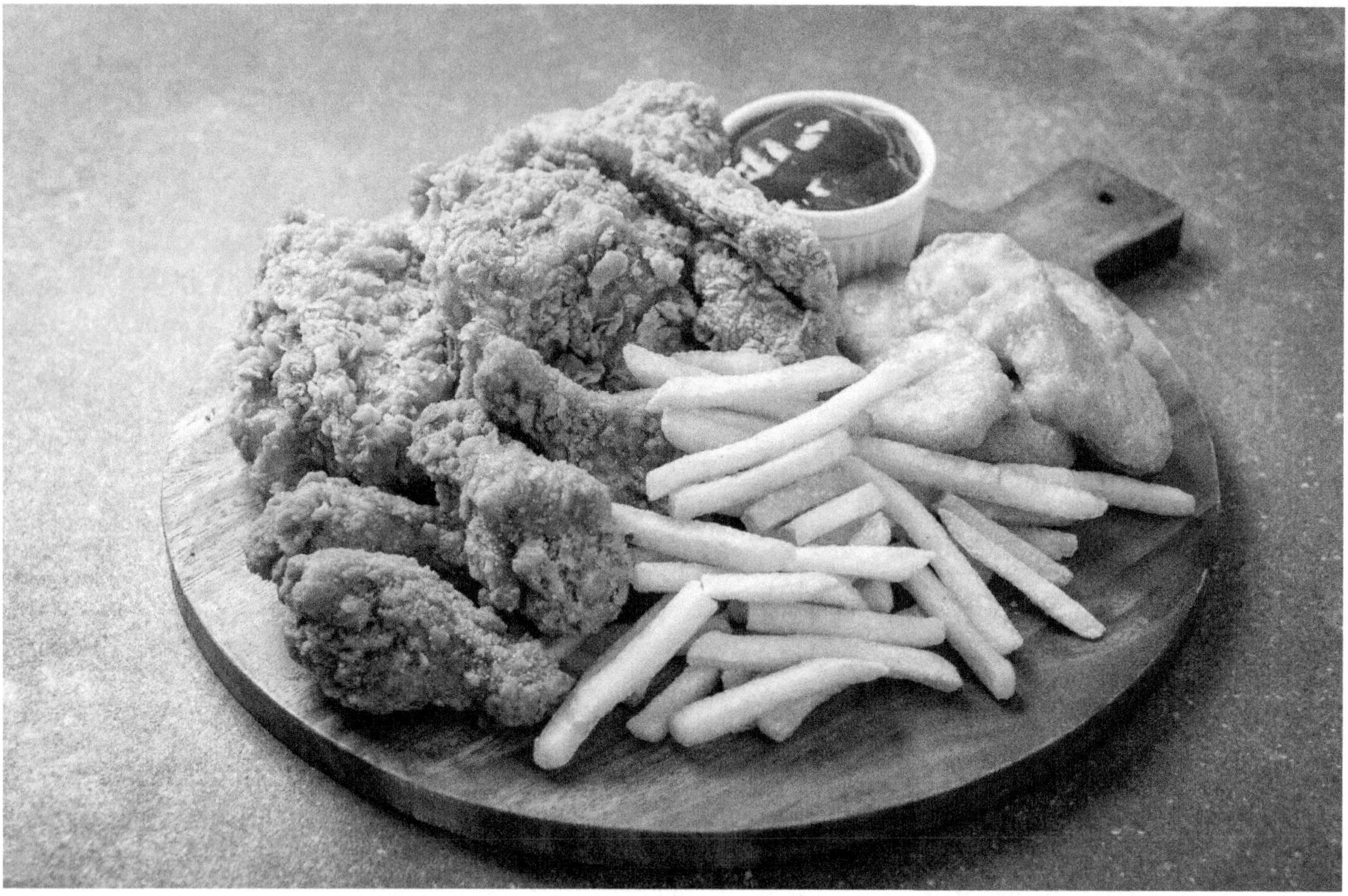

BREAKFAST

Air Fryer Toad in The Hole

Prep Time: 4 mins
Cook Time: 4 mins
Total Time: 8 mins
Servings: 2

Ingredients;
- 2 slices bread
- 10 ml butter
- 2 eggs
- 30 g cheddar cheese shredded
- salt and pepper to taste

Preparation:
1. Preheat the air fryer to 170° C.
2. Using the bottom of a measuring cup, make a 5 cm hole in the centre of the loaf. Butter both sides of the bread.
3. Cook for 6-7 minutes after cracking the egg into the pressed-in circle. Depending on how runny you prefer your eggs, you may need an extra minute or two.
4. During the last 2 mins of cooking, add the shredded cheese.

Nutrition information:
Calories 209 Carbs 14g Protein 11g Fat 12g Cholesterol 183 mg Fibre 1g Sugar 2g

Air Fryer English Breakfast

Prep Time: 3 mins
Cook Time: 15 mins
Total Time: 18 mins
Servings: 2

Ingredients:
- 6 English Sausages
- 6 Bacon Rashers
- 2 Large Tomatoes
- 4 Black Pudding
- ½ Can Baked Beans
- 2 Large Eggs
- 15 ml Whole Milk
- 5 g Butter
- Salt & Pepper

Preparation:
1. Crack the eggs into a ramekin and whisk in the butter, milk, salt, and pepper. Put it in the air fryer. Add bacon rashers, black pudding, and sausages to the air fryer. Cut tomatoes in half and season with salt and pepper on top.
2. Close the air fryer basket, ensuring sure that each of the breakfast items has enough area to cook. Then bake for 10 minutes at 180 degrees Celsius. However, at the 5-minute mark, mix your eggs with a fork.
3. When the air fryer sounds, check to see if the eggs are scrambled and remove them with a kitchen glove or tongs. Replace one of the ramekins with cold baked beans.

Cook for 5 minutes more at the same temperature.
4. When it beeps, dish your English breakfast components, and serve.

Nutrition information:
Calories 1496, Carbs 22g, Protein 70g, Fat 124g, Cholesterol 463mg, Fibre 6g, Sugar: 4g

Cheesy Baked Eggs

Prep Time: 4 mins
Cook Time: 16 mins
Servings: 2

Ingredients:
- 4 large Eggs
- 60 g Smoked gouda, chopped
- Everything bagel seasoning
- salt and pepper to taste

Preparation:
1. Cooking sprays the insides of each ramekin. Fill each ramekin with 2 eggs and 28 g of chopped gouda. Season with salt and pepper to taste. Top each ramekin with you are everything bagel seasoning (as much as you like).
2. Put one ramekin in the air fryer basket. Cook for 16 minutes at 205° C or until the eggs are cooked through. Serve.

Nutrition information:
Calories: 240kcal Carbohydrates: 1g Protein: 12g Fat: 16g

Sausage Breakfast Casserole

Prep Time: 10 mins
Cook Time: 20 mins
Total Time: 30 mins
Servings: 6

Ingredients:
- 450 g Hash Browns
- 450 g Ground Breakfast Sausage
- 1 Green Bell Pepper Diced
- 1 Red Bell Pepper Diced
- 1 Yellow Bell Pepper Diced
- 10 g Sweet Onion Diced
- 4 Eggs

Preparation:
1. Line the air fryer basket with foil.
2. Place the hash browns on the bottom of the pan.
3. Serve with the uncooked sausage on top.
4. Arrange the peppers and onions evenly on top.
5. Cook for 10 minutes at 180 degrees Celsius.
6. If necessary, open the air fryer and stir the dish.

7. Crack each egg into a basin, then pour over the casserole.
8. Cook for another 10 mins at 180°C.
9. Season to taste with salt and pepper.

Nutrition information:
Calories 517 Carbs 27g Protein 21g Fat: 37g Fat 25g Fibre: 3gSugar: 4g

Banana Nut Bread

Prep Time: 10 mins
Cook Time: 45 mins
Total Time: 55 mins
Servings: 12 Slices

Ingredients:
- 80 g softened butter
- 130 g natural cane sugar or brown sugar
- 5 ml vanilla extract
- 2 medium eggs
- 220 g mashed bananas or 2 large bananas mashed
- 150 g all-purpose flour
- 5 g sodium bicarbonate
- 5 g ground cinnamon
- 1.5 g salt
- 90 g walnuts chopped

Preparation:
1. Beat the softened butter & sugar together until the butter becomes pale.
2. Add the eggs one at a time, then beat well after each addition. Add vanilla essence and mashed bananas and stir just until combined.
3. Fold in the flour, baking powder, baking soda, and cinnamon to the liquid ingredients until thoroughly blended and no flour lumps remain. Add 60 g of walnuts.
4. Pour the batter into a 20 cm x 10 cm loaf pan that has been oiled and lined with parchment paper. On top, sprinkle with the remaining walnuts and brown sugar. Cover it with foil and puncture it numerous times with a knife.
5. Preheat the Air Fryer for 3 min at 160 degrees Celsius. In the basket, place the covered loaf pan and bake for 40 min, or until a skewer inserted into the centre comes out clean.
6. Take out the foil and continue baking at 120 degrees Celsius for another 5 minutes to brown the top.
7. Allow the basket to cool after removing it from the Air fryer. Let the banana bread cool on a cutting board. Cut into slices and serve.

Nutrition information:
Calories 170 Carbs 27 g Protein 2.5 g Fat 6 g Fibre 1 g

Oatmeal Casserole

Preparation time: 10 minutes
Cooking time: 20 minutes
Servings: 8

Ingredients:
- 500 g rolled oats
- 4 g Bicarbonate of soda
- 70 g demerara sugar
- 5 g cinnamon powder
- 80 g chocolate chips cookies
- 70 g blueberries
- 1 banana, peeled and mashed

- 450 ml milk
- 1 egg
- 30 g butter
- 5 ml vanilla extract
- Cooking spray

Preparation:
1. In a mixing bowl, combine sugar, bicarbonate of soda, cinnamon, chocolate chips, blueberries, and banana.
2. Whisk together the eggs, vanilla extract, and butter in a separate bowl.
3. Preheat your air fryer to 160°C, then treat the bottom with frying spray and layer with oats.
4. Cook for 20 minutes after adding the cinnamon-egg mixture.
5. Before dividing it into dishes and dishing it for breakfast, give it one last good stir.

Nutritional information: calories 300, fat 4g, fibre 7g, carbs 12g, protein 10g

Basic Air Fryer Hot Dogs

Prep Time: 5 mins
Cook Time: 5 mins
Total Time: 10 mins
Servings: 4

Ingredients:
- 4 hot dog buns
- 4 hot dogs

Preparation:
1. Preheat an air fryer to 200° C.
2. Place the buns in your air fryer basket in a single layer and cook until crisp, about 2 minutes. Place the buns on a platter.
3. Cook the hot dogs in your air fryer basket in a single layer for 3 minutes. Hot dogs should be served in toasted buns.

Nutrition information:
calories 269 fat 15 g cholesterol 24 mg carbs 23g fibre 1g sugars 4g protein 9g

Quick Vegan Air Fryer Garlic Bread

Prep time 3 mins
Cooking time 5 mins
Total time 8 mins
Servings 4

Ingredients:
- 4 mini wheat tortillas
- 60 g vegan butter (or vegan spread)
- 2 large cloves of garlic
- 1.5 g dried parsley (or fresh, chopped)
- 1 generous pinch of chilli flakes
- 1 pinch salt and pepper

Preparation:
1. Peel and smash the garlic or grate it coarsely.

2. Soften the butter in a basin using the back of a spoon.
3. After adding the garlic, herbs, and chilli, season with salt and pepper.
4. Thoroughly combine.
5. Distribute the mixture evenly across four mini wheat tortillas.
6. In an air fryer, bake for 5 minutes at 180° C. Keep an eye on it, and if you have shelves, change them out since the top one cooks more quickly.
7. Before serving, cut into triangles.

Nutritional information: Calories: 88kcal Carbohydrates: 1g Protein: 0.2g Fat: 9g

Mushroom Quiche

Prep time: 10 minutes
Cook time: 10 minutes
Servings: 4

Ingredients:
- 20 ml flour
- 15 g butter, soft
- 22 cm pie crust
- 2 button mushrooms, chopped
- 40 g ham, chopped
- 3 eggs
- 1 small yellow onion, chopped
- 80 g double cream
- A pinch of nutmeg, ground
- Salt and black pepper to the taste
- 2.5 g thyme, dried
- 60 g Swiss cheese, grated

Preparation:
1. Flour your work surface and roll out the pie dough.
2. Press it into the bottom of your air fryer's pie plate.
3. Whisk together the butter, mushrooms, Ham, onion, eggs, double cream, salt, pepper, thyme, and nutmeg in a mixing bowl.
4. Spread mixture over the pie shell, then top with Swiss cheese and set the pie pan in the air fryer.
5. Cook your quiche for 10 minutes at 200° C.
6. Cut into slices and serve for breakfast.

Nutritional information: calories 212, fat 4g, fibre 6g, carbs 7g, protein 7g

Scrambled Eggs

Preparation time: 10 minutes
Cooking time: 10 minutes
Servings: 2

Ingredients:
- 2 eggs
- 30 g butter
- Salt and black pepper to the taste
- 1 red pepper, chopped
- A pinch of sweet paprika

Preparation:

1. In a mixing bowl, combine eggs, salt, pepper, paprika, and red pepper.
2. Preheat the air fryer to 70° C, then add the butter and melt it.
3. After adding the egg mixture, cook for 10 minutes.
4. For breakfast, arrange scrambled eggs on plates.

Nutritional information: calories 200, fat 4g, fibre 7g, carbs 10g, protein 3g

Garlic Potatoes with Bacon

Prep time: 10 minutes
Cook time: 20 minutes
Servings: 4

Ingredients:
- 4 peeled and cut into medium cubes potatoes
- 6 minced garlic cloves
- 2 rosemary springs, chopped 4 bacon slices
- 15 ml olive oil
- To taste, season with salt and black pepper.
- 2 whisked eggs

Preparation:
1. Combine the oil, potatoes, garlic, bacon, rosemary, salt, pepper, and eggs in the pan of your air fryer.
2. Cook the potatoes at 200° C for 20 minutes before dividing them among plates and serving for breakfast.

Nutritional information:
calories 211, fat 3g, fibre 5g, carbs 8g, protein 5g

Turkey Burrito

Prep time: 10 minutes
Cook time: 10 minutes
Servings: 2

Ingredients:
- 4 slices turkey breast already cooked
- ½ red pepper, sliced
- 2 eggs
- 1 small avocado, peeled, pitted and sliced
- 40 g salsa
- Salt and black pepper to the taste
- 250 g mozzarella cheese, grated
- Tortillas for serving

Preparation:
1. In a mixing bowl, whisk the eggs with salt and pepper to taste, then pour them into a pan and set it in the air fryer basket.
2. Cook for 5 minutes at 200° C before removing the pan from the fryer and placing eggs on a platter.

3. Distribute the eggs, turkey meat, red pepper, cheese, salsa, and avocado among the tortillas on a work surface.
4. Roll your burritos and lay them in an air fryer coated with tin foil.
5. Heat the burritos for 3 minutes at 150° C before dividing them onto plates and serving.

Nutritional information: calories 349, fat 23g, fibre 11g, carbs 20g, protein 21g

Dates and Millet Pudding

Prep time: 10 minutes
Cook time: 15 minutes
Servings: 4

Ingredients:
- 400 ml milk
- 200 ml water
- 150 g millet
- 4 dates pitted
- Honey for serving

Preparation:
1. Place the millet in an air fryer-safe pan, add the dates, milk, and water, mix, and cook at 180 degrees Celsius for 15 minutes.
2. Divide among dishes and sprinkle with honey before serving for breakfast.

Nutritional information: calories 231, fat 6g, fibre 6g, carbs 18g, protein 6g

Air Fryer Veggie Sandwich

Prep Time: 5 Mins
Cook Time: 10 Mins
Total Time: 15 Mins
1 sandwich

Ingredients:
- A handful of grated cheese
- A few red pepper slices
- A few mushroom slices
- 1 cherry tomato, quartered
- A large spoonful of pesto
- 2 slices of bread
- little olive oil (for spritzing the bread)

Preparation:
1. First, brush the peppers and mushrooms with oil and air fry for five minutes at 200°C.
2. Assemble your sandwich. Before packing the bread with cheese, pepper, tomato, and mushrooms, spread pesto on both sides.
3. The outside of the bread should be coated or drizzled with olive oil. Top the sandwich with a bit more cheese.
4. Air fryr the bread in an air fryer at 200° C for 5 minutes or until it is golden and crispy.

Nutritional information: Calories: 491 Carbs 35g Protein 16g Fat 32g Fiber 2g Sugar 5g

Eggs Casserole

Prep time: 10 minutes
Cook time: 25 minutes
Servings: 6

Ingredients:
- 450 g turkey, ground
- 15 ml olive oil
- 5 g chilli seasoning mix
- 12 eggs
- 1 sweet potato, cubed
- 30 g baby spinach
- Salt and black pepper to the taste
- 2 tomatoes, chopped for serving

Preparation:
1. In a mixing dish, combine the eggs, salt, pepper, chilli spice mix, potato, spinach, turkey, and sweet potato.
2. Preheat your air fryer to 180°C before adding the oil and heating it.
3. Cover and cook the egg mixture in the air fryer for 25 minutes.
4. Serve on separate plates for breakfast.

Nutritional information; calories 300, fat 5g, fibre 8g, carbs 13g, protein 6g

Long Beans Omelette

Prep time: 10 minutes
Cook time: 10 minutes
Servings: 3

Ingredients:
- 3 ml Worcestershire sauce
- 15 ml olive oil
- 3 eggs, whisked
- A pinch of salt and black pepper
- 4 garlic cloves, minced
- 4 long beans, trimmed and sliced

Preparation:
1. In a mixing bowl, combine eggs, salt, black pepper, and Worcestershire sauce.
2. Preheat your air fryer to 160°C, then add the oil and garlic and stir for 1 minute.
3. After adding the long beans and egg mixture, cook for 10 minutes.
4. For breakfast, serve the omelette on plates.

Nutritional information: calories 200, fat 3g, fibre 7g, carbs 9g, protein 3g

Ham Breakfast Pie

Prep time: 10 minutes
Cook time: 25 minutes
Servings: 6

Ingredients:
- 450 g Puff pastry
- 2 eggs, whisked
- 450 g Gouda Cheese, grated
- 15 g Sussex Charmer, grated
- 130 g cooked and chopped Ham
- Salt and black pepper to the taste
- Cooking spray

Preparation:
1. Preheat the air fryer to 180°C and coat it with frying spray.
2. Whisk together the eggs, Gouda Cheese, Sussex Charmer, salt, and pepper in a mixing dish, then pour over the puff pastry.

3. Spread the Ham on top, then cut the remaining crescent roll dough into strips and place them on top of the Ham. Bake for 25 minutes at 150° C.
4. Breakfast should be served with the pie.

Nutritional information:
calories 400, fat 27g, fibre 7g, carbs 22g, protein 16g

Air Fryer Monte Cristo Sandwich

Prep Time 15 mins
Cook Time 9 mins
Servings: 4

Ingredients:
- 8 slices bread
- 170 g pancake mix
- 1 egg
- 60 ml water
- 350 ml whole milk
- 16 slices ham
- 16 slices cheese Swiss, Gouda, or Gruyere

Preparation:
1. After 7 minutes at 190° C, your air fryer will be ready. Meanwhile, in a medium mixing bowl, combine the pancake mix, egg, milk, and water.
2. The water and milk should be gradually mixed until you get a thick pancake mixture; it should be thicker than your regular batter but not runny. Set aside.
3. Assemble the sandwiches as follows: On one piece of bread, layer two slices of cheese, four slices of Ham, two more slices of cheese, and the second piece of bread.
4. With your palm, gently press down on the sandwich. To keep the sandwich together, gently insert four toothpicks at an angle along each edge of the bread. By this time, the air fryer should have finished preheating, so place a paper liner inside the basket and close the lid without turning it back on.
5. The sandwich should be well covered with pancake batter on one side before gently flipping over and coating on the other. Lifting and allowing the additional batter to flow off the step should not be skipped. Then, on top of the liner paper, place the air fryer basket.
6. Set a timer for 7 minutes at 190° C. Flip the item over and set the temperature and timing to 180° C and 1 minute, respectively, to finish browning and to fry the second side. Remove the sandwiches from the air fryer, remove the toothpicks, keep them warm by wrapping them in aluminium foil, and allow the sandwiches to cool fully.
7. To serve, cut each sandwich in half, sprinkle with powdered sugar, and serve with a few numbers of raspberry preserves for dipping. Enjoy!

Nutritional information:
Calories 980 Carbs 40g Protein 63g Fat 62g Fiber 3g Sugar 6g

Tuna and Courgette Tortillas

Prep time: 10 minutes
Cook time: 10 minutes

Servings: 4

Ingredients:
- 4 corn tortillas
- 30 g butter, soft
- 170 g canned tuna, drained
- 120 g Courgette, shredded
- 80 g mayonnaise
- 30 g mustard
- 240 g cheddar cheese, grated

Preparation:
1. Spread butter on tortillas and cook for 3 minutes at 200° C in an air fryer basket.
2. Meanwhile, in a mixing bowl, combine the tuna, courgette, mayo, and mustard.
3. Split the mixture among the tortillas, top with cheese, roll the tortillas, and set them in the air fryer basket for 4 minutes at 200° C.
4. Serve.

Nutritional information:
Calories 162, fat 4g, fibre 8g, carbs 9g, protein 4g

Air Fryer French Bread Pizza

Prep Time: 5 minutes
Cook Time: 9 minutes
Total Time: 14 minutes
Servings: 4

Ingredients:
- 350 g loaf of French bread
- 15 ml olive oil
- 1.5 g oregano
- 1 g garlic powder
- 120 ml pizza sauce
- 12 slices of mozzarella or provolone cheese or 166 g of shredded cheese
- 12 slices of pepperoni cut into fourths (optional)

Preparation:
1. Preheat the air fryer to 190° C if required.
2. To produce two long pieces, split the French bread loaf in half lengthwise. By splitting each component, you may make four pieces.
3. In a small mixing bowl, mix the olive oil, oregano, and garlic powder. Apply a thin coating of pastry cream on the cut side of the French bread pieces in an even layer.
4. Place the seasoned French bread in the basket or tray of your air fryer, working in batches as required. Simply toast the bread at 190 degrees Celsius for 3 minutes.
5. Remove the air-fried French bread from the fryer. Before adding the cheese slices, evenly pour the pizza sauce over each piece. Pepperoni slices and other favourite toppings should be evenly spread on the pizzas.
6. Return the pizzas to the air fryer, working in batches if required, and cook for an additional 5 to 6 minutes at 190° C or until the cheese is melted.
7. Allow the pizzas to cool for a few minutes before serving.

Nutritional information:
Calories 433 Carbs 47g Protein 20g Fat 19g Fiber 2g Sugar 5g

BEEF, PORK, AND LAMB

Air Fryer Cornish Pasties

Prep Time: 5 mins
Cook Time: 8 mins
Total Time: 13 mins
Servings: 3

Ingredients:
- 200 g Leftover Instant Pot Beef Stew
- 500 g Air Fryer Pie Crust
- Egg Wash
- 5 g Mixed Herbs
- Salt & Pepper

Preparation:
1. Load leftover beef stew into a bowl, draining any liquid, and season with salt, pepper, and mixed herbs.
2. Roll out your pastry, then cover it with the bottom of the pastry machine and cut out your rounds. You may need to roll again to acquire three pasty circles. As you make the pasty circles, lay them on a floured work surface.
3. After you've finished creating the pasty circles, insert one at a time into a pastry cutter. Fill one half of the pasty with the stew contents, being careful not to overfill it.
4. Push down, ensuring sure the lovely pasty pattern is left. Rinse and repeat until all of your pasties are finished.
5. Then, line the air fryer basket with foil and brush the top of the pastries with egg wash.
6. Before serving, air fried for 8 minutes at 200°C.

Nutrition information:
Calories 860 Carbs 81g Protein 25g Fat: 47g Cholesterol 41mg Fiber 4g Sugar 1g

Pork Chops and Mushrooms Mix

Prep time: 10 minutes
Cook time: 40 minutes
Servings: 3

Ingredients:
- 220 g mushrooms, sliced
- 5 g garlic powder
- 1 yellow onion, chopped
- 220 g mayonnaise
- 3 pork chops, boneless
- 5 g nutmeg
- 15 ml balsamic vinegar
- 120 ml olive oil

Preparation:

1. Heat the oil in an air fryer-compatible frying-pan over moderate heat, then add the mushrooms and onions, combine, and cook for 4 minutes.
2. Brown the pork chops on all sides in the nutmeg and garlic spice mixture.
3. Cook for 30 minutes at 165° Celsius in an air fryer.
4. Before plating, mix in the vinegar and mayonnaise.

Nutritional information:
Calories 600, fat 10 g, fibre 1 g, carbs 8g, protein 30g

Pork Chops and Sage Sauce

Prep time: 10 minutes
Cook time: 15 minutes
Servings: 2

Ingredients:
- 2 pork chops
- Salt and black pepper to the taste
- 15 ml olive oil
- 30 g butter
- 1 shallot, sliced
- 1 handful of sage, chopped
- 5 ml lemon juice

Preparation:

1. Season the pork chops with salt & pepper, massage with the oil, and cook for 10 minutes at 185° C, flipping halfway through.
2. Meanwhile, melt the butter in a frying-pan over medium heat, then add the shallot and cook for 2 minutes, swirling constantly.
3. Simmer for a few minutes more after adding the sage and lemon juice, then remove from heat.
4. Serve the pork chops with sage sauce drizzled all over.

Nutritional information:
Calories 265, fat 6 g, fibre 8 g, carbs 19 g, protein 12 g

Easy Air Fryer Pork Chops

Prep Time: 5 mins
Cook Time: 20 mins
Total Time: 25 mins
Servings: 4

Ingredients:
- 50 g grated Parmesan cheese
- 5 g paprika
- 5 g garlic powder
- 5 g kosher salt
- 5 g dried parsley
- 2 g ground black pepper
- 4 (150 g) boneless pork chops
- 30 ml extra virgin olive oil

Preparation:
1. Preheat the air fryer to 190° C.
2. On a flat, shallow plate, combine the Parmesan cheese, paprika, garlic powder, salt, parsley, and pepper; stir thoroughly.
3. Apply olive oil to each pork chop. Place each chop on a platter and dredge both sides in the Parmesan mixture.
4. Place 2 chops in the air fryer basket and cook for 10 minutes, turning halfway through.

5. Transfer to a chopping board and set aside for 5 minutes to rest. Rep with the remaining chops.

Nutrition information:
calories 305 fat 17g cholesterol 90mg sodium 685mg carbs 2g protein 35g

Air Fryer Bone-In Pork Chops with Breading

Prep Time 5 minutes
Cook Time 8 minutes
Total Time 13 minutes
Servings: 2 Pork Chops

Ingredients:
- 2 bone-in pork chops, centre-cut (thin OR thick)
- 2 tablespoons mayonnaise or Miracle Whip
- 130 g Italian breadcrumbs
- 2 g garlic powder
- 2 g onion powder
- 2 g thyme
- 1.5 g salt
- pinch of paprika
- pepper, to taste

Preparation:
1. Trim excess fat from the pork chops as needed, then warm the air fryer to 200°C.
2. In a shallow, flat basin, combine the breadcrumbs, thyme, salt, paprika, garlic powder, onion powder, and pepper.
3. Brush the pork chops lightly with mayonnaise or Miracle Whip before coating them in the breadcrumb mixture to evenly coat all sides.
4. In the air fryer, cook the breaded pork chops for 8 to 10 minutes, rotating them gently halfway through. Cook for 14-15 minutes if making thicker pork chops.
5. Remove the pork chops from your air fryer and serve!

Nutritional information:
Calories 494 Fat 24 Cholesterol 135 mg carbs:22 fibre 2g sugar 2g protein 45g

Ginger Pork Skewers (Air Fryer or Grill)

Prep Time: 10 mins
Cook Time: 10 mins
Marinating Time: 30 mins
Total Time: 50 mins
Servings: 3

Ingredients:
- 450 g pork shoulder
- 30 g ginger, peeled and sliced, then crushed (about 20 ml of crushed ginger)
- ½ tablespoon crushed garlic
- 70 ml soy sauce
- 20 ml honey (or more to taste)
- 20 ml rice vinegar
- 8 ml toasted sesame oil
- 8 skewers
- cucumber sticks (to serve)

Preparation:
1. Cut the meat into 6 mm thick slices. To tenderize the pork, pound it briefly with a pestle or meat mallet (flat side). Place in a mixing bowl.

2. In a small bowl, combine the ginger, garlic, soy sauce, honey, rice vinegar, and sesame oil. Taste and adjust to your liking. Pour 2/3 of the marinade over the meat and save the rest to baste it as it cooks.
3. Marinate the pork for 25-30 minutes at room temperature in the marinade. After that, thread onto skewers.
4. Preheat your air fryer to 180°C, as directed by the manufacturer. Cook for 5-6 minutes with the skewers in the basket. Then, remove the pork skewers from the air fryer and brush both sides with the leftover marinade before cooking for another 2-3 minutes, or until the meat is completely cooked.
5. Alternatively, grill (or grill pan) the skewers for several minutes until thoroughly done. Before grilling, lightly oil the grates and baste the pork with the saved marinade.
6. Serve immediately with cucumber sticks (and, if desired, rice) on the side.

Nutrition information:
Calories 213 Carbs 12g Protein 21g Fat 9g Cholesterol 62mg Fiber 1g Sugar 9g

Air Fryer Sausage

Prep Time 2 mins
Cook Time 10 mins
Total Time 11 mins

Servings: 4

Ingredients:
- 4-5 Italian sausage links
- parchment paper (optional)

Preparation:
1. Fill the air fryer basket halfway with sausage links. To collect any grease, line the bottom of the air fryer basket with parchment paper.
2. 10-12 minutes at 200°C, or until golden brown on the exterior and juicy on the interior. Uncooked sausages should have an internal temperature of 65°C when properly cooked. Serve hot, if preferred.

Nutrition Information:
Calories 323 Fat 26g cholesterol 53mg sodium 697mg carbs 4g fibre 0g sugar 2g protein 18g

Beef Casserole

Prep time: 30 minutes
Cook time: 35 minutes
Servings: 12

Ingredients:
- 15 ml olive oil
- 900 g beef, ground
- 170 g Aubergine, chopped
- Salt and black pepper to the taste
- 10 g mustard
- 10 ml gluten-free Worcestershire sauce
- 800 g canned tomatoes, chopped
- 450 g mozzarella, grated
- 300 ml ketchup
- 8 g parsley, chopped
- 5 g oregano, dried

Preparation:
1. To coat, combine the aubergine, salt, pepper, and oil in a mixing dish.

2. Combine the meat, salt, pepper, mustard, and Worcestershire sauce in a separate dish; stir well and place in the bottom of an air fryer pan.
3. Finally, combine the aubergine mixture, tomatoes, ketchup, parsley, oregano, and mozzarella in a mixing bowl.
4. In your air fryer, cook for 35 minutes at 180 degrees Celsius.
5. Serve right away on plates.

Nutritional information: calories 200, fat 12, fibre 2, carbs 16, protein 15

Balsamic Beef

Preparation time: 10 minutes
Cooking time: 1 hour
Servings: 6

Ingredients:
- 1 medium beef roast
- 15 ml Worcestershire sauce
- 120 ml balsamic vinegar
- 200 ml beef stock
- 15 ml honey
- 15 ml soy sauce
- 4 garlic cloves, minced

Preparation:
1. In a heatproof dish that fits your air fryer, combine the roast with the Worcestershire sauce, vinegar, stock, honey, soy sauce, and garlic, stir well, and cook for 1 hour at 190 degrees C.
2. Divide the roast among plates and sprinkle with the sauce.

Nutritional information: calories 311, fat 7, fibre 12, carbs 20, protein 16

Air Fryer Meatloaf

Prep Time: 10 mins
Cook Time: 25 mins
Additional Time: 10 mins
Total Time: 45 mins
Servings: 4

Ingredients:
- 450 g lean minced beef
- 1 small onion, finely chopped
- 1 large egg, lightly beaten
- 20 g dry breadcrumbs
- 15 g chopped fresh thyme
- 5 g salt
- ground black pepper to taste
- 2 mushrooms, thickly sliced
- 15 ml olive oil, or as needed

Preparation:
1. Preheat an air fryer to 200° C.
2. In a mixing bowl, combine minced beef, onion, bread crumbs, thyme, egg, salt, and pepper. Knead and completely combine. Place the mixture in a small loaf pan. Smooth the top, then push in the mushrooms and drizzle with olive oil.
3. Cook the meatloaf in the preheated air fryer for about 25 minutes or until well browned. A thermometer put into the middle should read at least 75 degrees Celsius.
4. Allow the meatloaf to rest for upto 10 mins before cutting it into wedges and serving.

Nutrition information:
calories 297 fat 19g carbs 6g fibre 1g sugars 1g protein 25g

Beef and Green Onions Marinade

Prep time: 10 minutes
Cook time: 20 minutes
Servings: 4
Ingredients:
- 100 g green onion, chopped
- 240 ml soy sauce
- 120 ml water
- 50 g brown sugar
- 60 ml sesame seeds
- 5 garlic cloves, minced
- 5 g black pepper
- 450 g lean beef

Preparation:
1. In a mixing bowl, combine the onion, soy sauce, water, sugar, garlic, sesame seeds, and pepper. Toss in the meat and leave aside for 10 minutes.
2. Drain the steak and cook it for 20 minutes at 200° C in your preheated air fryer.
3. Slice, divide among plates, and serve with a side salad.

Nutritional information: Calories 329, fat 8 g, fibre 12 g, carbs 26 g, protein 22 g

Beef Kabobs

Prep time: 10 minutes
Cook time: 10 minutes
Servings: 4

Ingredients:
- 2 red peppers, chopped
- 1 kg sirloin steak, cut into medium pieces
- 1 red onion, chopped
- 1 Courgette, sliced
- Juice from 1 lime
- 15 g chilli powder
- 30 ml hot sauce
- 5 ml cumin, ground
- 60 ml olive oil
- 70 ml salsa
- Salt and black pepper to the taste

Preparation:
1. Combine salsa, lime juice, oil, hot sauce, chilli powder, cumin, salt, and black pepper in a mixing bowl.
2. Divide the pork, peppers, courgette, and onion among skewers, spray with the salsa mixture you made earlier, and cook for 10 minutes at 190° C, turning kabobs halfway through.
3. Serve on separate dishes with a side salad.

Nutritional information: calories 170, fat 5, fibre 2, carbs 13, protein 16

Tender Air Fryer Steak with Garlic Mushrooms

Prep Time 5 mins
Cook Time 15 mins
Total Time 20 mins
Servings: 2

Ingredients:
- 15 ml Avocado Oil
- 450 g Ribeye Steaks
- 500 g Halved Fresh Mushrooms
- 2.5 g Salt
- 2 g Black Pepper
- 35 g Unsalted Butter (Melted)
- 3 Cloves Minced Garlic
- 1.5 g Red Pepper Flakes (Optional)

- Chopped Parsley (Optional Garnish)

Preparation:
1. Preheat your Air Fryer to 210°C for 4 minutes.
2. Pat the steaks dry before cutting them into 12 mm cubes. In a large mixing bowl, combine the steak cubes.
3. In a large mixing bowl, combine the cubed steak and cut the fresh mushrooms in half.
4. In a large mixing bowl, combine the steak chunks and mushrooms with the melted butter, garlic, salt, pepper, and red pepper flakes.
5. Place the mixture in an air fryer basket in an even, non-overlapping layer.
6. The steak and mushrooms were air-fried for 7-15 minutes, turning twice throughout that period. Check the steak after 7 minutes to see whether it's done to your liking. If it's still too pink, keep cooking.
7. Garnish with parsley and serve immediately for the best flavour and texture.

Nutritional information: Calories 663 Carbs 5g Protein 49g Fat 51g Cholesterol 168mg Fiber 1g Sugar 2g

Air Fryer Hamburger Stuffed Mushrooms

Prep Time: 10 mins
Cook Time: 12 mins
Total Time: 22 mins

Servings: 2

Ingredients:
- 2 large portobello mushrooms
- 170 g ground beef
- 1.25 g salt
- 1.25 g garlic powder
- 1.25 g ground black pepper
- 5 ml melted butter
- Hamburger toppings: lettuce, tomato, pickle, cheese, ketchup, mustard, mayo

Preparation:
1. Remove the portobello mushroom stems.
2. Combine the ground beef, salt, garlic powder, and black pepper in a mixing bowl. Make two circular patties from the meat that will fit within the mushrooms.
3. Fill the mushroom with ground beef.
4. Preheat the air fryer to 180° C for 3-5 minutes. Lightly coat the basket with oil. Cook the mushrooms in the basket for 6 minutes. Open the basket and brush the tops and sides of the packed mushrooms with butter.
5. Cook for an additional 6 minutes. With 1 minute left, add a piece of cheese for the top to melt (any longer, and it might slide off the top).
6. Remove the filled mushrooms from the basket. Garnish with your favourite garnishes.

Nutritional information:
Calories 254 Carbs 4g Protein 16g Fat 19g Cholesterol 66mg Fiber 1g Sugar 2g

Lamb and Lemon Sauce

Preparation time: 10 minutes
Cook time: 30 minutes
Servings: 4

Ingredients:
- 2 lamb shanks
- Salt and black pepper to taste
- 2 garlic cloves, minced

- 60 ml olive oil
- Juice from ½ lemon
- Zest from ½ lemon
- 2.5 g oregano, dried

Preparation:
1. Season the lamb with salt and pepper, rub it with garlic, and cook it in an air fryer for 30 minutes at 180° C.
2. Meanwhile, in a mixing bowl, combine the lemon juice, zest, salt and pepper, olive oil, and oregano.
3. Remove bone, shred lamb, divide among plates, and serve with lemon dressing.

Nutritional information: calories 260, fat 7, fibre 3, carbs 15, protein 12

Lamb and Green Pesto

Preparation time: 1 hour
Cook time: 45 minutes
Servings: 4

Ingredients:
- 60 g parsley
- 30 g mint
- 1 small yellow onion, roughly chopped
- 50 g pistachios, chopped
- 5 ml lemon zest, grated
- 80 ml olive oil
- Salt and black pepper to the taste
- 1 kg lamb riblets
- ½ onion, chopped
- 5 garlic cloves, minced
- Juice from 1 orange

Preparation:
1. In a food processor, combine parsley, mint, onion, pistachios, lemon zest, salt, pepper, and oil until smooth.
2. Place the lamb in a medium bowl, cover it with plastic wrap, and refrigerate for 1 hour.
3. Transfer the lamb to an air fryer-compatible baking dish, add the garlic and cook for 45 minutes at 160° C.
4. Serve the lamb on separate plates.

Nutritional information: Calories 200, fat 4 g, fibre 6 g, carbs 15 g, protein 7 g

Lamb and Spinach Mix

Preparation time: 10 minutes
Cook time: 35 minutes
Servings: 6

Ingredients:
- 12 g ginger, grated
- 2 garlic cloves, minced
- 4 g cardamom, ground
- 1 red onion, chopped
- 450 g lamb meat, cubed
- 10 g cumin powder
- 2 g chilli powder
- 2 g turmeric
- 10 g coriander, ground
- 450 g spinach
- 400 g canned tomatoes, chopped

Preparation:
1. In a heatproof dish that fits your air fryer, combine the lamb, spinach, tomatoes, ginger, garlic, onion, cardamom, cloves, cumin, garam masala, chilli, turmeric, and

coriander, and cook at 180° C for 35 minutes.
2. Serve in separate bowls.

Nutritional information: calories 160, fat 6, fibre 3, carbs 17, protein 20

3. Cook the rosemary, carrots, and lamb ribs in the air fryer for 30 minutes at 175° C.
4. Serve the lamb mixture on dishes that have been heated.

Nutritional information: calories 302, fat 7, fibre 2, carbs 22, protein 27

Tasty Lamb Ribs

Prep time: 15 minutes
Cook time: 40 minutes
Servings: 8

Ingredients:
- 8 lamb ribs
- 4 garlic cloves, minced
- 2 carrots, chopped
- 500 g veggie stock
- 15 g rosemary, chopped
- 30 ml extra virgin olive oil
- Salt and black pepper to the taste
- 25 g white flour

Preparation:
1. Season lamb ribs with salt and pepper, massage with oil and garlic, and cook for 10 minutes in a preheated air fryer at 190° C.
2. In a heatproof dish large enough to hold your fryer, combine the stock and flour.

Lamb Roast and Potatoes

Prep time: 10 minutes
Cook time: 45 minutes
Servings: 6

Ingredients:
- 1.8 kg lamb roast
- 1 spring rosemary
- 3 garlic cloves, minced
- 6 potatoes, halved
- 120 ml lamb stock
- 4 bay leaves
- Salt and black pepper to the taste

Preparation:
1. Put potatoes in an air fryer-safe dish, add lamb, garlic, rosemary spring, salt, pepper, bay leaves, and stock, stir, and cook at 190° C for 45 minutes.
2. Serve lamb slices on plates with potatoes and cooked juice.

Nutritional information: calories 273, fat 4, fibre 12, carbs 25, protein 29

Spicy Lamb Sirloin Steak

Prep Time: 40 mins
Cook Time: 20 mins
Servings: 4

Ingredients:
- 450 lamb sirloin steaks, pastured, boneless

For the Marinade:
- 1/2 white onion, peeled
- 5 g ground fennel
- 5 garlic cloves, peeled
- 4 slices ginger
- 5 g salt
- 5 g garam masala
- 5 g ground cassia
- 5 g cayenne pepper

Preparation:
1. In a food processor, combine all marinade ingredients and pulse until thoroughly combined.
2. Cut the lamb chops with a knife, then place them in a large mixing bowl with the marinade.
3. Refrigerate the lamb chops for at least 30 minutes after properly coating them with the marinade.
4. Then, turn on the air fryer, insert the frying basket, coat with olive oil, close the cover, and warm for 5 minutes at 170° C.
5. Open the fryer, place the lamb chops inside, cover, and cook for 15 minutes, or until the steaks are golden brown and done, flipping midway through.
6. When the air fryer beeps, transfer the lamb steaks to a dish and serve.

Nutritional information:
Calories: 181 Carbs: 3 g Fat: 7 g Protein: 23 g Fiber: 1 g

Herbed Lamb Chops

Prep Time: 1h 10 mins
Cook Time: 13 mins
Servings: 4

Ingredients:
- 450 g lamb chops, pastured

For the Marinate:
- 2 tbsp. lemon juice
- 5 g dried rosemary
- 5 g salt
- 5 g dried thyme
- 5 g coriander
- 5 g dried oregano
- 30 ml olive oil

Preparation:
1. In a mixing bowl, whisk together all the marinade ingredients.
2. Place the lamb chops in a large plastic bag, add the marinade, close the bag, and flip the bag upside down to coat the lamb chops with the marinade. Refrigerate for approximately one hour before serving.
3. Then, turn on the air fryer, insert the fryer basket, coat it with olive oil, close the cover, and warm for 5 minutes at 200°C.
4. Close the cover on the fryer, add the marinated lamb chops, and cook for 8 minutes, or until golden brown and done, flipping halfway through.
5. Transfer the lamb chops to a serving dish and serve when the air fryer beeps.

Nutritional information:
Calories: 177 Carbs: 1.7 g Fat: 8 g Protein: 23 g
Fiber: 0.5 g

POULTRY RECIPES

Shepherd's Pie in Air Fryer

Prep Time: 20 minutes
Cook Time: 10 minutes
Total Time: 30 minutes
Servings: 4

Ingredients
- 340 g boneless, skinless chicken breasts
- 1.5 g salt plus extra for sprinkling
- 1.5 g black pepper plus extra for sprinkling
- 340 g jar chicken gravy
- 270 g frozen mixed vegetables thawed
- 2.5 g onion powder
- 420 g prepared mashed potatoes
- 30 g butter melted

Preparation
1. Cooking sprays the air fryer basket. Season the chicken with salt & Pepper, then set it in the air fryer basket for 5 minutes. Cook for 5 to 6 minutes more or until no pink remains in the middle of the chicken. Transfer to a cutting board and cool slightly before cutting into 13 mm portions.
2. Meanwhile, cook the gravy, veggies, onion powder, 1,5 g salt, and 1.5 g pepper in a pan over medium heat. Cook for 5 to 7 mins or until well cooked. When the chicken is done, toss it in and divide the mixture evenly among four (1-cup) ramekins.
3. Drizzle melted butter over each ramekin of 105 g mashed potatoes.

Nutrition information
Calories 356 Carbs: 38g Protein 23g Fat 13g Fiber 5g Sugar 2g

Chicken Pizza Crust

Prep Time: 10 minutes
Cook Time: 25 minutes
Serving: 4

Ingredients:
- 454 g ground chicken thigh meat
- 22 g grated Parmesan cheese
- 112 g shredded mozzarella

Preparation
1. In a large mixing basin, combine all the ingredients. Cut into four equal halves.
2. Each portion of the chicken mixture should be spread out onto one of the four 15 cm parchment circles. As required, place into the air fryer basket in batches.
3. Set the air fry to 190°C and set the timer for 25 minutes.
4. Halfway through the cooking process, flip the crust.
5. When it is sufficiently done, add the cheese and any toppings and simmer for another five minutes. You may also freeze or chill the crust and top it until ready to serve.

Nutritional information:
Calories: 230 Protein: 24.7 g fibre: 0.0 g fat: 13 g Carbs 1.2 g Sugar 0.2 g

Air Fryer Orange Chicken

Prep Time: 5 minutes
Cook Time: 15 minutes
Total Time: 20 minutes
Servings: 2

Ingredients
- 450 g boneless skinless chicken breasts or chicken thighs
- 15 g corn-starch or potato starch

For The Orange Sauce
- 120 ml orange juice
- 25 g brown sugar
- 15 ml soy sauce
- 15 ml rice wine vinegar
- 1.5 g of ground ginger
- dash of red pepper flakes
- zest of one orange
- 10 ml corn-starch mixed with 10 ml water

Optional To Serve
- green onions, chopped
- sesame seeds

Preparation
1. Preheat the air fryer to 200 degrees Celsius.
2. Combine the chicken pieces and cornflour in a mixing bowl until evenly coated (see notes above about not overcoating them).
3. Cook, shaking the basket halfway through, for 7-9 mins, or until the chicken achieves an internal temperature of 80 degrees Celsius.
4. Meanwhile, combine the orange juice, brown sugar, rice wine vinegar, soy sauce, ginger, red pepper flakes, and orange zest in a small saucepan over medium heat.
5. Bring the mixture to a boil, then continue to simmer for 5 minutes.
6. Combine cornflour and water in a separate bowl and stir into the orange sauce.
7. Allow to boil for one minute more, constantly stirring, before removing from heat.
8. Toss the chicken with the sauce after removing it from the air fryer.
9. Garnish with green onions & sesame seeds before serving if desired.

Nutritional information
Calories 630 Fat 15 g Cholesterol 193 mg carbs 46g fibre 4g sugar 22g protein 75g

Air Fryer Chicken Katsu and Homemade Katsu Sauce

Prep Time: 20 mins
Cook Time: 20 mins
Total Time: 40 mins
Servings: 4

Ingredients
Katsu Sauce:

- 100 ml ketchup
- 30 ml soy sauce
- 15 g brown sugar
- 15 ml sherry
- 10 ml Worcestershire sauce
- 5 g minced garlic

Chicken:
- 450 g boneless skinless chicken breast, sliced in half horizontally
- 1 pinch salt
- ground black pepper to taste
- 2 large eggs, beaten
- 150 g panko bread crumbs
- cooking spray

Preparation
1. Make the sauce: In a mixing bowl, combine ketchup, soy sauce, brown sugar, sherry, Worcestershire sauce, and garlic until the sugar is dissolved. Set aside the katsu sauce.
2. Preheat an air fryer to 175° C.
3. Meanwhile, place the chicken in a clean work area. Season with salt and Pepper to taste.
4. In a flat plate or shallow bowl, place the beaten eggs. Fill a second flat plate halfway with bread crumbs. Dredge the chicken in the egg, then in the bread crumbs. Repeat by dredging the chicken in egg, then bread crumbs, pushing down to ensure the bread crumbs adhere to the chicken.
5. Place the chicken pieces in the preheated air fryer basket. Non-stick cooking spray should be sprayed on the tops.
6. Ten minutes in the air fryer. Using a spatula, flip the chicken pieces over and coat the tops with non-stick cooking spray. Cook for another 8 minutes. Slice the chicken on a cutting board. Serve with katsu sauce on the side.

Nutritional information:
calories 318 fat 7g cholesterol 158 mg carbs 41 g sugars 11g protein 32g

Air Fryer Coconut Chicken

Prep Time: 10 mins
Cook Time: 10 mins
Additional Time: 2 h
Total Time: 2 h 20 mins
Servings: 4

Ingredients
- 120 ml canned coconut milk
- 120 ml pineapple juice
- 25 g brown sugar
- 15 ml soy sauce
- 10 ml Sriracha sauce
- 5 g ground ginger
- 450 g boneless skinless chicken breasts cut into strips
- 2 eggs
- 100 g sweetened shredded coconut
- 120 g panko bread crumbs
- 8 g salt
- 2.5 g ground black pepper
- Non-stick cooking spray

Preparation
1. In a medium mixing bowl, combine the coconut milk, pineapple juice, brown sugar, Sriracha sauce, soy sauce, and ginger. Toss in the chicken strips to coat. Refrigerate for 2 hours or overnight, covered with plastic wrap.
2. Preheat an air fryer to 190° C.
3. In a mixing dish, whisk together the eggs. In a separate dish, combine the shredded coconut, panko, salt, and Pepper.
4. Shake off any excess marinade from the chicken strips. Remove the leftover marinade and set aside. Dip chicken strips in the beaten egg, in the coconut-panko mixture, then back in the egg mixture, and finally in the coconut-panko mixture, dipping and coating each strip twice.
5. Cooking spray should be sprayed on the air fryer basket.
6. Place the breaded chicken strips in the air fryer basket, not touching; work in batches if required.

7. Cook for 6 minutes, then rotate the strips and cook for another 4 to 6 minutes or until gently browned and toasted.

Nutrition information
calories 418 fat 17g cholesterol 158mg carbs 41g fibre 3g sugars 17g protein 31g

Air Fryer Chicken Piccata with Lemon-Caper Sauce

Prep Time: 20 mins
Cook Time: 30 mins
Total Time: 50 mins
Servings: 4

Ingredients
Lemon-Caper Sauce:
- 60 g unsalted butter
- 4 cloves garlic, minced
- 16 g all-purpose flour
- 120 ml chicken broth
- 120 ml dry white wine
- 60 ml fresh lemon juice
- 30 g capers, drained
- 15 g finely chopped fresh parsley
- 5 g lemon zest
- 2.5 g kosher salt
- 1 g black pepper

Chicken Piccata:
- Non-stick cooking spray
- 2 (227 g) skinless, boneless chicken breast halves
- 60 g all-purpose flour
- 1 large egg
- 15 ml fresh lemon juice
- 15 ml freshly grated Parmesan cheese
- 15 ml freshly grated Asiago cheese
- 15 ml freshly grated Pecorino Romano cheese
- 120 g seasoned bread crumbs
- 7 g ground black pepper
- 5 g kosher salt

Preparation:
1. The lemon-caper sauce is prepared as follows: Melt the butter in a saucepan on medium heat. Cook for about a minute, occasionally stirring, until the garlic is aromatic. About 2 minutes of continuous whisking cooking will result in a minor mixture thickening.
2. With the chicken broth, white wine, and lemon juice, bring to a boil. Add the capers, parsley, lemon zest, salt, and Pepper after turning off the heat. When ready to use, cover and preheat. Gently whisk before serving.
3. Chicken should be prepared as follows: To begin using an air fryer, preheat it for 10 minutes at 200°C, as directed by the manufacturer. Spray some non-stick spray gently on the air fryer basket.
4. Cut each chicken breast in half lengthwise. The chicken breast halves should be placed on a large chopping board that has been lined with plastic wrap. Each chicken breast piece should be pounded to a 12 mm thickness.
5. Flour and baking powder should be combined in a medium mixing dish. The egg and lemon juice should be combined in a second medium mixing dish. Cheese and bread crumbs should be combined in a third medium mixing bowl. Sprinkle the chicken breast halves with equal amounts of salt and Pepper.

6. Work in batches as you dredge the chicken in flour until it is completely covered. Toss lightly to coat in the egg mixture before coating once more in the breadcrumbs mixture. Set in a baking pan. Continue until you have breaded all the chicken.
7. Place two pieces of breaded chicken in the fryer basket that has been heated. A thermometer inserted into the thickest portion should read 90° C after cooking for 8 to 10 minutes or until the food is golden brown and crispy. Halfway through cooking, turn the chicken pieces over and recoat the top. The leftover chicken is cooked and placed on a platter.
8. Along with the lemon-caper sauce, serve right away.

Nutrition information:
calories 491 fat 19g cholesterol 147 mg carbs 40g fibre 3g sugars 3g protein 34g

Air Fryer Maple Chicken Thighs

Prep Time: 10 mins
Cook Time: 25 mins
Additional Time: 1 hrs
Total Time: 1 hrs 35 mins
Servings: 4

Ingredients
- 240 ml buttermilk
- 120 ml maple syrup
- 1 egg
- 5 g granulated garlic
- 4 skin-on, bone-in chicken thighs

Dry Mix:
- 60 g all-purpose flour
- 40 g tapioca flour
- 15 g salt
- 5 g sweet paprika
- 2.5 g smoked paprika
- 5 g granulated onion
- 1.2 g ground black pepper
- 1.2 g cayenne pepper
- 2.5 g granulated garlic
- 2.5 g honey powder

Preparation
1. In a resealable bag, combine buttermilk, maple syrup, egg, and 5 g granulated garlic. Marinate the chicken thighs for up to 1 hour or up to overnight in the refrigerator.
2. In a shallow bowl, combine flour, tapioca flour, salt, sweet paprika, smoked paprika, granulated onion, Pepper, Cayenne Pepper, 2.5 g granulated garlic, and honey powder.
3. Preheat an air fryer to 190° C.
4. Take out the chicken thighs from the marinade and set them aside. Dredge the chicken in the flour mixture and brush off any excess. Cook the chicken for 12 minutes, skin side down, in a preheated air fryer. Fry the thighs for a further 13 minutes.

Nutrition information
calories 415 fat 13g cholesterol 113 mg carbs 51g fibre 1g sugars 27g protein 23g

Crumbed Chicken Tenderloins (Air Fried)

Prep Time: 15 mins
Cook Time: 15 mins
Total Time: 30 mins
Servings: 4

Ingredients:
- 1 large egg
- 75 g dry bread crumbs
- 30 ml vegetable oil
- 8 chicken tenderloins

Preparation:
1. Preheat an air fryer to 180° C.
2. In a small bowl, whisk the egg. In a separate dish, combine bread crumbs and oil until the mixture is loose and crumbly.
3. Dip each chicken tenderloin into the egg, shaking off any excess. Dip the chicken into the crumb mixture, coating it evenly and completely. Arrange the chicken tenderloins in an equal layers in the air fryer basket.
4. Cook until the centre is no longer pink, approximately 12 minutes. A thermometer put into the middle should read at least 85 degrees Celsius.

Nutrition information:

calories 253 fat 11g cholesterol 109 mg carbs 10g fibre 1g sugars 1g protein 26g

Air Fryer Chicken and Waffle Kabobs

Prep Time: 15 mins
Cook Time: 15 mins
Total Time: 30 mins
Servings: 4

Ingredients:
- 16 pieces frozen popcorn chicken
- 1 Kg frozen mini waffles
- 20 (10 cm to 15 cm) wooden skewers
- 150 g halved fresh strawberries
- 50 g fresh blueberries
- 40 g fresh raspberries

Preparation:
1. Preheat an air fryer to 200° C.
2. Arrange the popcorn chicken in the air fryer basket in a single layer. Cook for 7 mins, then turn and cook for another 2 to 3 minutes or until lightly browned and crispy. Place the chicken pieces on a baking pan and keep warm in a preheated air fryer.
3. Meanwhile, stack half of the waffles in the air fryer basket in a single layer. Cook for 90 seconds, then turn and cook for another 20 seconds or until light brown in places and crispy. Place on a baking sheet. Rep with the remaining waffles.
4. Thread 2 waffles and 2 chicken pieces onto each of 8 skewers. Thread the remaining 12 skewers with berries.

Nutrition information:

calories 517 fat 21g cholesterol 34 mg carbohydrate 71g fibre 11g protein 26g

Air Fryer Blackened Chicken Breasts

Prep Time: 10 mins
Cook Time: 20 mins
Additional Time: 10 mins
Total Time: 40 mins
Servings: 2

Ingredients:
- 10 g paprika
- 5 g ground thyme
- 5 g cumin
- 2.5 g cayenne pepper
- 2.5 g onion powder
- 2.5 g black pepper
- 1.5 g salt
- 10 ml vegetable oil
- 2 (170 g) skinless, boneless chicken breast halves

Preparation:
1. In a mixing bowl, combine paprika, thyme, cumin, cayenne Pepper, onion powder, black Pepper, and salt; transfer to a big plate.
2. Rub oil over each chicken breast until well covered, then push into the spice mixture to coat all sides. Place the basket in the air fryer.
3. Preheat the air fryer for 5 mins at 190 degrees Celsius.
4. Air-fry the chicken for about 10 minutes or until no longer pink in the middle and the juices flow clearly. A thermometer put into the middle should read at least 85 degrees Celsius.
5. Place the chicken on a platter and let it aside for 5 minutes before serving.

Nutrition information:
calories 245 fat 7g cholesterol 99mg carbs 3g fibre 2g protein 40g

Air Fryer Sesame Chicken Thighs

Prep Time: 5 mins
Cook Time: 15 mins
Additional Time: 35 mins
Total Time: 55 mins
Servings: 2

Ingredients:
- 30 ml sesame oil
- 30 ml soy sauce
- 15 ml honey
- 15 ml sriracha sauce
- 5 ml rice vinegar
- 908 g chicken thighs
- 1 green onion, chopped
- 20 g toasted sesame seeds

Preparation:
1. In a large mixing bowl, combine sesame oil, soy sauce, honey, sriracha, and vinegar. Stir in the chicken to mix. Refrigerate for at least 30 minutes, covered.
2. Preheat an air fryer to 200° C. Remove the chicken from the marinade.
3. Place the skin-side-up chicken thighs in the air fryer basket. 5 minutes in the oven. Cook for another 10 minutes on the other side.
4. Place the chicken on a platter and let it aside for 5 minutes before serving. Garnish with green onion and sesame seeds if desired.

Nutrition information:
calories 485 fat 33g cholesterol 141mg carbs 7g fibre 1g sugars 5g protein 40g

Air Fryer BBQ Cheddar-Stuffed Chicken Breasts

Prep Time: 10 mins
Cook Time: 25 mins
Total Time: 35 mins
Servings: 2

Ingredients:
- 3 strips bacon, divided
- 60 g Cheddar cheese, cubed, divided
- 60 ml barbeque sauce divided
- 2 (120 g) skinless, boneless chicken breasts
- salt and ground black pepper to taste

Preparation:
1. Preheat an air fryer to 190° C. In the air fryer, cook 1 strip of bacon for 2 minutes. Take out of the air fryer and chop into little pieces. Preheat your air fryer to 200 degrees Celsius and line the basket with parchment paper.
2. In a mixing bowl, combine cooked bacon, Cheddar cheese, and 15 ml barbecue sauce.
3. To make a little internal pouch, make a horizontal 2.5 cm cut at the top of each chicken breast using a long, sharp knife. Stuff each breast evenly with the bacon-cheese mixture. Wrap each chicken breast in the remaining bacon pieces. Coat the chicken breast with the leftover barbecue sauce and drop it in the air fryer basket.
4. Cook for 10 minutes in the air fryer, then turn and cook for another 10 mins, or until the chicken is no pinker on the inside and the juices run clear. A thermometer put into the middle should read at least 90 degrees Celsius.

Nutrition information:
calories 379 fat 19g cholesterol 114 mg carbs 12g sugars 8g protein 38g

Air Fryer Bacon-Wrapped Stuffed Chicken Breasts

Prep Time: 15 mins
Cook Time: 30 mins
Total Time: 45 mins
Servings: 3

Ingredients:
- 3 skinless, boneless chicken breasts
- 5 ml lemon-pepper seasoning, or to taste
- 3 slices Monterey Jack cheese
- 6 spears fresh asparagus

- 9 slices bacon
- 12 wooden toothpicks

Preparation:
1. Preheat the air fryer to 185°C per the manufacturer's instructions.
2. Using paper towels, pat the chicken pieces dry. Butterfly the breasts by cutting them horizontally across the middle with a sharp knife, starting at the thickest area and not cutting all the way through to the other side. Spread the two sides out as if they were a book.
3. Both sides should be seasoned with lemon-pepper spice. Put 1 piece of cheese on each chicken breast. Cut the asparagus spears in half and arrange four halves on top of the cheese. Roll the chicken up and over the cheese and asparagus, tucking it within each roll. Wrap three pieces of bacon around each chicken breast, using wooden toothpicks to secure the bacon where it overlaps.
4. Air-fry each bacon-wrapped breast for 15 minutes in the air fryer basket. Cook for another 15 minutes. Check the doneness of the chicken; an instant-read thermometer placed into the centre should read 90 degrees C.

Nutrition information:
calories 393 fat 23g cholesterol 123 mg carb 2g fibre 1g sugars 1g protein 42g

Pecan Crusted Chicken

Prep Time: 5 mins
Cook Time: 12 mins
Total Time: 17 mins
Servings: 4

Ingredients
- 450 g chicken tenders
- 5 g Sea Salt
- 5 g Ground Black Pepper
- 2.5 g Smoked Paprika
- 60 g Coarse-Ground Mustard
- 30 ml Sugar-Free Maple Syrup or honey
- 80 g finely-crushed pecans

Preparation
1. Place the chicken tenders in a large mixing basin.
2. Combine the salt, Pepper, and smoked paprika in a mixing bowl until the chicken is well coated.
3. Mix in the honey and mustard well.
4. Scatter the finely broken pecans on a plate.
5. Roll each chicken piece in the crumbled pecans until both sides are coated. With a brush, remove any excess.
6. Place the tenders in your air fryer basket and repeat until all the tenders are coated and in the air fryer basket.
7. Preheat the air fryer to 190 degrees Celsius for 12 minutes or until the chicken is done and the pecans are golden brown.

Nutritional information
Calories 325 Carbs 8g Protein 27g Fat 21g Fiber 3g Sugar 3g

Cornish Hen in Air Fryer (Super Easy)

Prep Time 10 mins
Cook Time 30 mins
Total Time 40 mins
Serving: 2

Ingredients:
- 5 g onion powder
- 5 g garlic powder
- 5 g paprika
- 2.5 g dry rosemary
- 2.5 g dry thyme
- 1 Kg Cornish hen
- 15 ml olive oil or avocado oil
- Salt and Pepper to taste

Preparation:

1. Preheat your air fryer for 5 mins at 200 degrees Celsius.
2. In a medium bowl, combine the onion powder, garlic powder, paprika, rosemary, and thyme.
3. Pat the cornish hen dry with a paper towel. Season the Cornish hen, including the cavity, with salt and Pepper to taste, and then rub the spice mix all over the bird, including the cavities and below the skin.
4. Cook the cornish game hen for 20 minutes breast side down and 10 minutes breast side up in the air fryer basket at 200° C. The cornish hen should be cooked until the internal temperature reaches 85 degrees Celsius.
5. Allow 10 minutes for the Cornish hen to rest before slicing. Enjoy

Nutrition Information:
Calories 135 Fat 14g Carbs 3g Fiber 1g Sugar 0g Protein 1g

Air Fryer Lemon Pepper Wings

Prep Time 5 mins
Cook Time 25 mins
Total Time 30 mins
Serving: 4

Ingredients:
- 600 g chicken wings, drumettes and flats separated and tips discarded
- 10 ml lemon pepper seasoning
- 1 g cayenne pepper

For The Lemon Pepper Sauce
- 40 g butter
- 5 ml lemon pepper seasoning
- 5 ml honey

Preparation:
1. Preheat your air fryer to 200 degrees Celsius.
2. Lemon pepper and cayenne pepper season the chicken wings.
3. Fill the air fryer up to halfway with lemon pepper wings. Cook, shaking halfway through, for 20-22 minutes.
4. Cook for a further 3-5 minutes at 200 degrees Celsius to get a nice crispy exterior on the chicken wings.
5. As the chicken wings are cooking, mix the melted butter, additional lemon pepper spice, and honey in a dish.

6. Remove the chicken wings from your air fryer and drizzle with the lemon honey sauce.

Nutrition Information:
Calories: 462 Fat: 36g Cholesterol: 154 mg Carbs: 2g fibre: 0g Sugar: 1g Protein: 31g

FISH & SEAFOOD RECIPES

Air Fryer Fish & Chips

Prep Time: 5 minutes
Cook Time: 10 minutes
Total Time: 15 minutes
Servings: 4 servings

Ingredients
- 60 g all-purpose flour
- 10 g paprika
- 2.5 g garlic powder
- 2.5 g salt
- 1.2 g black pepper
- 1 Large egg beaten
- 50 g panko bread crumbs
- 450 g cod fillet cut into strips
- Cooking oil spray
- Tartar sauce for serving
- Lemon wedges for serving

Preparation
1. Combine the flour, paprika, garlic powder, salt, and black pepper in a small mixing bowl. In another dish, combine the beaten egg and the panko breadcrumbs.
2. Pat the fish dry with a paper towel. Dredge the fish in the flour-egg mixture, then in the panko breadcrumbs, pressing lightly to attach the crumbs. Apply oil on both sides.
3. Air fry at 200°C for 10-12 minutes, flipping halfway through, until crispy and faintly brown.
4. Open the basket and use a fork to examine if the appropriate doneness peels off easily. If required, return the fish for another 1 or 2 minutes.
5. Serve immediately with fries and, if wanted, tartar sauce.

Nutrition information
Calories 200 Carbohydrates 18g Protein 24g Fat 2g Cholesterol 90mg

Roasted Cod and Prosciutto

Prep time: 10 minutes
Cook time: 10 minutes
Servings: 4

Ingredients:
- 4 g parsley, chopped
- 4 medium cod filets
- 50 g butter, melted
- 2 garlic cloves, minced
- 30 ml lemon juice
- 50 g prosciutto, chopped

- 5 g Dijon mustard
- 1 shallot, chopped
- Salt and black pepper to the taste

Preparation
1. In a mixing bowl, combine mustard, butter, garlic, parsley, shallot, lemon juice, prosciutto, salt, and pepper.
2. Season the fish with salt & pepper, then cover with the prosciutto mixture and cook in your air fryer for 10 minutes at 210° C.
3. Serve on separate plates.

Nutritional information: calories 200, fat 4g, fiber 7g, carbs 12g, protein 6g

Air-Fryer Fish Cakes

Prep Time: 10 mins
Total Time: 20 mins
Servings: 2

Ingredients
- Non-stick cooking spray
- 300 g finely chopped white fish (such as grouper, catfish, or cod)
- 60 g breadcrumbs
- 10 g finely chopped coriander
- 20 ml chili sauce
- 30 ml mayonnaise
- 1 large egg
- 1.2 g salt
- 2.5 g ground pepper
- 2 lime wedges

Preparation
1. Coat your air fryer basket with cooking spray.
2. Stir together the fish, breadcrumbs, coriander, chilli sauce, mayonnaise, egg, salt, and pepper in a medium mixing bowl. Make four 8 cm diameter cakes with the batter.
3. After spraying the cakes with cooking spray, place them in the prepared basket. Cook the cakes at 210° C for 9 to 10 minutes, or until browned and the internal temperature reaches 70°C. Lime wedges are optional.

Nutritional information:
Calories 399 Fat 16g Carbs 28g Protein 35g

Air Fryer Mahi Mahi with Brown Butter

Prep Time: 5 mins
Cook Time: 15 mins
Total Time: 20 mins

Ingredients
- 4 (200 g) mahi mahi fillets
- salt and ground black pepper to taste
- cooking spray
- 120 g butter

Preparation
1. Preheat the air fryer to 190° Celsius.
2. Mahi Mahi fillets are seasoned with salt and pepper before being coated on both sides with frying spray. When placing the fillets in the air fryer basket, make sure to allow enough space between them.
3. Cook the fish for 12 minutes in a preheated air fryer, or until it flakes easily with a fork and turns golden.

4. Meanwhile, melt the butter in a small sauce pan over medium heat for 3 - 5 minutes, or until it foams and turns a deep brown colour. Take out the heat.
5. Brown butter should be poured over the fish fillets on a dish.

Nutritional information:
calories 416 total fat 32g saturated fat 20g protein 32g

2. Combine the oil, paprika, garlic powder, lemon juice, and lemon pepper in a mixing bowl. Coat the shrimp well.
3. Cook the shrimp for 6 to 8 minutes in a preheated air fryer, or until the flesh is opaque and the shrimp are vivid pink on the exterior. Serve with lemon wedges.

Nutritional information:
calories 215 total fat 9g total carbohydrate 13g dietary fiber 6g protein 29g

Air Fryer Lemon Pepper Shrimp

Prep Time: 5 mins
Cook Time: 10 mins
Total Time: 15 mins

Ingredients
- 15 ml olive oil
- 1 lemon, juiced
- 5 g lemon pepper
- 1.2 g paprika
- 1.2 g garlic powder
- 350 g uncooked medium shrimp, peeled and deveined
- 1 lemon, sliced

Preparation
1. Preheat an air fryer to 200 degrees Celsius according the manufacturer's instructions.

Salmon and Avocado Salsa

Preparation time: 30 minutes
Cooking time: 10 minutes
Servings: 4

Ingredients:
- 4 salmon fillets
- 15 ml olive oil
- Salt and black pepper to the taste
- 5 g cumin, ground
- 5 g sweet paprika
- 2 g chili powder
- 5 g garlic powder

For the salsa:
- 1 small red onion, chopped
- 1 avocado, pitted, peeled, and chopped
- 5 g Coriander, chopped

- Juice from 2 limes
- Salt and black pepper to the taste

Preparation
1. In a bowl, combine salt, pepper, chilli powder, onion powder, paprika, and cumin; stir. Rub salmon with this mixture; sprinkle with oil; rub again; and cook at 185° C for 5 minutes on each side.
2. Meanwhile, in a mixing dish, combine the avocado, red onion, salt, pepper, coriander, and lime juice.
3. Serve the fillets with the avocado salsa on plates.

Nutritional information: calories 300, fat 14g, fiber 4g, carbs 18g, protein 16g

Halibut and Sun-Dried Tomatoes Mix

Preparation time: 10 minutes
Cooking time: 10 minutes
Servings: 2

Ingredients:
- 2 medium halibut fillets
- 2 garlic cloves, minced
- 10 ml olive oil
- Salt and black pepper to the taste
- 6 sun-dried tomatoes, chopped
- 2 small red onions, sliced
- 1 fennel bulb, sliced
- 10 black olives, pitted and sliced
- 4 rosemary springs, chopped
- 5 g red pepper flakes, crushed

Preparation
1. Season the fish with salt & pepper, then massage it in a heat-resistant dish that fits your air fryer with garlic and oil.
2. Cook for 10 minutes at 200° C with onion slices, sun-dried tomatoes, fennel, olives, rosemary, and pepper flakes in your air fryer.
3. Separately plate the fish and veggies.

Nutritional information: calories 300, fat 12g, fiber 9g, carbs 18g, protein 30g

Coconut Tilapia

Prep time: 10 minutes
Cook time: 10 minutes
Servings: 4

Ingredients:
- 4 medium tilapia fillets
- Salt and black pepper to the taste
- 120 ml coconut milk
- 2 g ginger, grated
- 15 g Coriander, chopped
- 2 garlic cloves, chopped
- 1 g garam masala
- Cooking spray
- ½ jalapeno, chopped

Preparation:
1. In a food processor, combine coconut milk, salt, pepper, coriander, ginger, garlic, jalapeno, and garam masala and pulse until smooth.
2. Cook for 10 minutes at 220° C after coating the fish with cooking spray and sprinkling it with the coconut mixture.
3. Serve right away on plates.

Nutritional information:
calories 200, fat 5g, fiber 6g, carbs 25g, protein 26g

Tuna and Chimichurri Sauce

Prep time: 10 minutes
Cook time: 8 minutes
Servings: 4

Ingredients:
- 30 g Coriander, chopped
- 80 ml olive oil
- 1 small red onion, chopped
- 40 ml balsamic vinegar
- 8 g parsley, chopped
- 3 g basil, chopped
- 1 jalapeno pepper, chopped
- 500 sushi tuna steak
- Salt and black pepper to the taste
- 5 g red pepper flakes
- 5 g thyme, chopped
- 3 garlic cloves, minced
- 2 avocados, pitted, peeled, and sliced
- 150 g mini arugula

Preparation
1. Whisk together 80 mL oil, jalapeno, vinegar, onion, Coriander, basil, garlic, parsley, pepper flakes, thyme, salt, and pepper in a mixing dish.
2. Season the tuna with salt and pepper, massage with the remaining oil, and fry for 3 minutes on each side at 190 degrees C.
3. To coat, toss the arugula with half of the chimichurri mixture.
4. Divide the arugula among the plates, then the tuna, ending with the leftover chimichurri and dishing.

Nutritional information:
calories 276, fat 3g, fiber 1g, carbs 14g, protein 20g

Air Fryer Lobster Tails with Lemon-Garlic Butter

Prep Time: 10 mins
Cook Time: 10 mins
Total Time: 20 mins

Ingredients
- 2 (120 g) lobster tails
- 50 g butter
- 5 g lemon zest
- 1 clove of garlic, grated
- salt and ground black pepper to taste
- 5 g chopped fresh parsley
- 2 wedges lemon

Preparation:
1. Preheat the air fryer to 210 degrees Celsius.
2. Butterfly lobster tails by cutting through the centres of the flesh and hard top shells longitudinally with kitchen shears. Cut up to but not past the bases of the shells. Distribute the tail sections. Place the lobster flesh, face up, in the air fryer basket with the tails.
3. Melt the butter in a medium saucepan over medium heat. Cook for 30 secs, or until the garlic is fragrant, with the lemon zest.
4. Transfer 30 g of the butter mixture to a small bowl and brush it onto the lobster

tails to prevent contamination from raw lobster. Remove any remaining butter. Season the lobster with salt and pepper.
5. Cook for 5 to 7 minutes in a preheated air fryer, or until the lobster flesh is opaque.
6. Pour the saved butter from the saucepan over the lobster flesh. Garnish with lemon wedges and parsley.

Nutritional information:
calories 313 fat 26g carbs 3g fiber 1g protein 18g

Air-Fryer Scallops with Lemon-Herb Sauce

Prep Time: 10 mins
Total Time: 20 mins
Servings: 2

Ingredients:
- 8 large (30 g.) sea scallops, cleaned and patted very dry
- 1.2 g ground pepper
- 1.5 g salt
- cooking spray
- 60 ml extra-virgin olive oil
- 8 g very finely chopped flat-leaf parsley
- 5 g capers, very finely chopped
- 2 g finely grated lemon zest
- 2.5 g finely chopped garlic
- lemon wedges, optional

Preparation
1. Add salt and pepper to the scallops before serving. Spray cooking oil on the basket of your air fryer. Spray frying spray on the basket before adding the scallops. In the fryer, put the basket. The scallops should be cooked at 220° C for 6 minutes, or until an internal temperature of 60° C is reached.
2. In a small bowl, mix the oil, parsley, capers, lemon zest, and garlic. On top of the scallops, drizzle. If desired, add lemon slices as a garnish.

Nutritional information:
Calories 348 Fat 30g Carbs 5g Protein 14g

Air Fryer Crab Rangoon

Prep Time: 15 mins
Cook Time: 20 mins
Total Time: 35 mins
Servings 4-6

Ingredients:
- 220 g package cream cheese, softened
- 100 g lump crab meat
- 12 g chopped scallions
- 5 ml soya sauce
- 5 ml Worcestershire sauce

- 1 serving non-stick cooking spray
- 24 wonton wrappers
- 30 ml Asian sweet chili sauce for dipping

Preparation:

1. Whisk together the cream cheese, crab meat, scallions, soy sauce, and Worcestershire sauce in a mixing bowl.
2. Preheat an air fryer to 175 degrees Celsius. The air fryer basket should be sprayed with cooking spray. A small basin should be filled with warm water.
3. On a clean work area, arrange 12 wonton wrappers. 5 g of the cream cheese mixture should be put in the centre of each wonton wrapper. Dip your index finger into warm water to wet the edges of each wonton wrapper. Crimp the wrapping corners upward until they converge in the centre to make dumplings.
4. Cooking spray the tops of the dumplings before placing them in the prepared basket.
5. Cook the dumplings for 8 to 10 minutes, or until they reach the desired crispness. Place on a dish lined with paper towels.
6. While the first batch is cooking, assemble the remaining dumplings using the remaining wrappers and filling.
7. Serve with sweet chilli sauce for dipping.

Nutritional information:
calories 127 total fat 7g carbs 11g sugars 1g protein 5g

Air Fried Seasoned Crunchy Cod Fillets

Prep Time: 10 mins
Cook Time: 12 mins
Total Time: 22 mins

Ingredients:
- avocado oil cooking spray
- 30 g unseasoned bread crumbs
- 50 g stone-ground yellow polenta.
- 6 g seasoning mix
- 5 g paprika
- 2 g salt, or to taste
- 120 ml buttermilk
- 3 (150 g) cod fillets
- 8 g plain flour

Preparation:
1. Create a 3-inch-wide foil sling that covers the bottom and sides of an air fryer in the basket form. Create a few holes in the foil sling's bottom that correspond to the holes in the basket. Spray the sling with avocado oil. If you're using a shelf-style air fryer, skip this step.
2. Preheat your air fryer to 200 degrees Celsius.
3. Combine the panko crumbs, yellow polenta, seasoning mix, paprika, and salt in a small bowl. In a separate basin, combine the buttermilk.
4. Pat dries the fish fillets with towels before gently sprinkling both sides with flour. Before coating with the crumb mixture, each flour-coated fillet should be dipped in buttermilk. Place each fillet on the foil sling or the rack of a shelf-style air fryer and coat with the crumb mixture on all sides. Spray each salmon fillet with avocado oil.
5. Cook for 10 to 12 minutes in an air fryer, or until the salmon flakes easily. The cod fillets should be removed from the air fryer using the sling and served immediately.

Nutritional information:
calories 224 fat 2g carbs 23g dietary fiber 1g sugars 2g protein 30g

Honey Sea Bass

Prep time: 10 minutes
Cook time: 10 minutes
Servings: 2

Ingredients:
- 2 sea bass fillets
- Zest from ½ orange, grated
- Juice from ½ orange
- A pinch of salt and black pepper
- 30 g mustard
- 10 ml honey
- 30 ml olive oil
- 220 g canned lentils, drained
- A small bunch of dill, chopped
- 60 g watercress
- A small bunch of parsley, chopped

Preparation
1. Season fish fillets with salt and pepper, add orange zest and juice, rub with 15 ml oil, honey, and mustard, massage, place in air fryer, and cook for 10 minutes at 180° C, turning halfway.
2. Meanwhile, in a medium saucepan over medium heat, boil the lentils, then add the remaining oil, watercress, dill, and parsley, toss well, and distribute among plates.
3. Serve with the fish fillets right away.

Nutritional information:
calories 212, fat 8g, fiber 12g, carbs 9g, protein 17g

VEGETARIAN RECIPES

Air Fried Leeks

Prep time: 10 minutes
Cook time: 7 minutes
Servings: 4

Ingredients:
- 4 leeks, washed and halved
- 15 g butter, melted
- 15 ml lemon juice
- Salt and black pepper to the taste

Preparation:
1. Rub leeks with frozen butter, season with salt and pepper, and cook in an air fryer for 7 minutes at 185° C.
2. Arrange on a plate and sprinkle with lemon juice before serving.

Nutritional information:
Calories 100, fat 4g, fibre 2g, carbs 6g, protein 2g

Beet Salad and Parsley Dressing

Prep time: 10 minutes
Cook time: 14 minutes
Servings: 4

Ingredients:
- 4 table beets
- 30 ml balsamic vinegar
- A bunch of parsley, chopped
- Salt and black pepper to the taste
- 15 ml extra virgin olive oil
- 1 garlic clove, chopped
- 15 g capers

Preparation:
1. Cook the table beets for 14 minutes at 190° C in your air fryer.
2. Meanwhile, in a mixing bowl, add parsley, garlic, salt, pepper, olive oil, and capers.
3. Cool the beets on a cutting board before peeling and slicing them into a salad dish.
4. Pour in the vinegar, followed by the parsley dressing, and serve.

Nutritional information:
Calories 70, fat 2g, fibre 1g, carbs 6g, protein 4g

Tomato and Basil Tart

Prep time: 10 minutes
Cook time: 14 minutes
Servings: 2

Ingredients:

- 1 bunch of basil, chopped
- 4 eggs
- 1 garlic clove, minced
- Salt and black pepper to the taste
- 100 g cherry tomatoes, halved
- 60 g cheddar cheese, grated

Preparation:
1. In a mixing bowl, combine the eggs, salt, black pepper, cheese, and basil.
2. Pour mixture into a baking dish that fits your air fryer, cover with tomatoes, and cook for 14 minutes at 170 degrees C.
3. After slicing, serve immediately.

Nutritional information:
Calories 140, fat 1g, fibre 1g, carbs 2g, protein 10g

Broccoli Salad

Prep time: 10 minutes
Cook time: 8 minutes
Servings: 4

Ingredients:
- 1 broccoli head, florets separated
- 15 ml peanut oil
- 6 garlic cloves, minced
- 15 ml Chinese rice wine vinegar
- Salt and black pepper to the taste

Preparation:
1. In a bowl, toss broccoli with salt, pepper, and half of the oil, then place in an air fryer and cook at 180° C for 8 minutes, shaking halfway through.
2. Serve the broccoli in a salad bowl with the remaining peanut oil, garlic, and rice vinegar.

Nutritional information:
Calories 121, fat 3g, fibre 4g, carbs 4g, protein 4g

Air Fried Asparagus

Prep time: 10 minutes
Cook time: 15 minutes
Servings: 4

Ingredients:
- 400 g fresh asparagus, trimmed
- 60 ml olive oil
- Salt and black pepper to the taste
- 5 g lemon zest
- 4 garlic cloves, minced
- 2 g oregano, dried
- 1 g red pepper flakes
- 100 g feta cheese, crumbled
- 8 g parsley, finely chopped
- Juice from 1 lemon

Preparation:
1. In a mixing bowl, combine the oil, lemon zest, garlic, pepper flakes, and oregano.
2. Toss in the asparagus, cheese, salt, and pepper, then transfer to an air fryer basket

and cook for 8 minutes at 190° C. Arrange asparagus on plates and top with parsley and lemon juice.

Nutritional information:
Calories 162, fat 13g, fibre 5g, carbs 12g, protein 8g

Courgette Noodles Delight

Prep time: 10 minutes
Cook time: 20 minutes
Servings: 6

Ingredients:
- 30 ml olive oil
- 3 Courgette cut with a spiralizer
- 500 g mushrooms, sliced
- 15 g sun-dried tomatoes, chopped
- 3 g garlic, minced
- 100 g cherry tomatoes, halved
- 300 g ketchup
- 60 g spinach, torn
- Salt and black pepper to the taste
- A handful of basil, chopped

Preparation:
1. Set aside for 10 minutes after seasoning the courgette noodles with salt and black pepper.
2. In a pan that fits your air fryer, heats the oil over medium-high heat, add the garlic, stir, and cook for 1 minute.
3. Stir in the mushrooms, sun-dried tomatoes, cherry tomatoes, spinach, cayenne pepper sauce, and courgette noodles before placing them in the air fryer for 10 minutes at 170° C.
4. Serve on plates, topped with a dusting of basil.

Nutritional information: calories 120, fat 1g, fibre 1g, carbs 2g, protein 9g

Brussels Sprouts and Butter Sauce

Prep time: 4 minutes
Cook time: 10 minutes
Servings: 4

Ingredients:
- 400 g Brussels sprouts, trimmed
- Salt and black pepper to the taste
- 120 g rashers cooked and chopped
- 15 g mustard
- 15 g butter
- 2 g dill, finely chopped

Preparation:
1. Cook Brussels sprouts for 10 minutes at 185 degrees Celsius in your air fryer.
2. Melt the butter in a skillet over medium-high heat, then add the rashers, mustard, and dill and thoroughly combine.
3. Serve Brussels sprouts on plates drizzled with butter sauce.

Nutritional information: calories 162, fat 8g, fibre 8g, carbs 14g, protein 5g

Spicy Cabbage

Prep time: 10 minutes
Cook time: 8 minutes
Servings: 4

Ingredients:

- 1 cabbage, cut into 8 wedges
- 15 ml sesame seed oil
- 1 carrot, grated
- 60 ml apple cider vinegar
- 60 ml apple juice
- 2 g cayenne pepper
- 5 g red pepper flakes, crushed

Preparation:
1. In a pan that fits your air fryer, combine cabbage, oil, carrot, vinegar, apple juice, cayenne pepper, and pepper flakes, mix, and cook at 190 degrees C for 8 minutes.
2. Plate up the cabbage mixture.

Nutritional information:
Calories 100, fat 4g, fibre 2g, carbs 11g, protein 7g

Delicious Portobello Mushrooms

Prep time: 10 minutes
Cook time: 12 minutes
Servings: 4

Ingredients:
- 10 basil leaves
- 40 g baby spinach
- 3 garlic cloves, chopped
- 100 g almonds, roughly chopped
- 4 g parsley
- 60 ml olive oil
- 8 cherry tomatoes, halved
- Salt and black pepper to the taste
- 4 Portobello mushrooms, stems removed and chopped

Preparation:
1. Combine basil, spinach, garlic, almonds, parsley, oil, salt, black pepper to taste, and mushroom stems in a food processor.
2. Stuff each mushroom with this mixture and cook for 12 minutes in an air fryer at 190° C.
3. Place the mushrooms on plates and serve.

Nutritional information:
Calories 145, fat 3g, fibre 2g, carbs 6g, protein 17g

Herbed Aubergine and Courgette Mix

Prep time: 10 minutes
Cook time: 8 minutes
Servings: 4

Ingredients:
- 1 Aubergine, roughly cubed
- 3 Courgette, roughly cubed
- 30 ml lemon juice
- Salt and black pepper to the taste
- 5 g thyme, dried
- 5 g oregano, dried
- 40 ml olive oil

Preparation:
1. Toss aubergine with Courgette, lemon juice, salt, pepper, thyme, oregano, and olive oil in an air fryer-safe dish, and cook at 190 degrees C for 8 minutes.
2. Serve on separate plates right away.

Nutritional information: calories 152, fat 5g, fibre 7g, carbs 19g, protein 5g

Stuffed Poblano Peppers

Preparation time: 10 minutes
Cooking time: 15 minutes
Servings: 4

Ingredients:
- 6 g garlic, minced
- 1 white onion, chopped
- 10 poblano peppers, tops cut off and deseeded
- 15 ml olive oil
- 250 g mushrooms, chopped
- Salt and black pepper to the taste
- 8 g Coriander, chopped

Preparation:
1. In a skillet over medium-high heat, heat the oil, then add the onion and mushrooms and cook for 5 minutes, stirring regularly.
2. After adding the garlic, coriander, salt, and black pepper cook for 2 minutes.
3. Divide the mixture among the poblanos and cook for 15 minutes at 180° C in an air fryer.
4. Serve on separate plates.

Nutritional information:
Calories 150, fat 3g, fibre 2g, carbs 7g, protein 10g

Radish Hash

Prep time: 10 minutes
Cook time: 7 minutes
Servings: 4

Ingredients:
- 5 ml onion powder
- 400 g radishes, sliced
- 5 g garlic powder
- Salt and black pepper to the taste
- 4 eggs
- 30 g parmesan, grated

Preparation:
1. Combine radishes, salt, pepper, onion and garlic powder, eggs, and parmesan in a mixing bowl.
2. Cook the radishes for 7 minutes at 180 degrees Celsius in an air fryer pan.
3. Serve the hash on separate plates.

Nutritional information:
Calories 80, fat 5g, fibre 2g, carbs 5g, protein 7g

Artichokes and Special Sauce

Prep time: 10 minutes
Cook time: 6 minutes
Servings: 2

Ingredients:
- 2 artichokes, trimmed
- A drizzle of olive oil
- 2 garlic cloves, minced
- 15 ml lemon juice

For the sauce:
- 60 ml coconut oil
- 60 ml extra virgin olive oil
- 3 anchovy fillets
- 3 garlic cloves

Preparation:
1. In a bowl, toss artichokes with oil, 2 garlic cloves, and lemon juice, then place in an air fryer and cook for 6 minutes at 185 degrees C. Distribute among plates.
2. In a food processor, combine coconut oil, anchovies, 3 garlic cloves, and olive oil until smooth. Drizzle over artichokes before serving.

Nutritional information: calories 261, fat 4g, fibre 7g, carbs 20g, protein 12g

Okra and Corn Salad

Preparation time: 10 minutes
Cooking time: 12 minutes
Servings: 6

Ingredients:
- 500 g okra, trimmed
- 6 spring onions chopped
- 3 green peppers, chopped
- Salt and black pepper to the taste
- 30 ml olive oil
- 5 g sugar
- 800 g canned tomatoes, chopped
- 120 g maize

Preparation:
1. In a pan large enough to fit your air fryer, heat the oil over medium-high heat, then add the spring onion and bell peppers, swirl, and cook for 5 minutes.
2. Stir in the okra, salt, pepper, sugar, tomatoes, and maize before cooking for 7 minutes at 190° C in the air fryer.
3. While the okra combination is still hot, serve it on plates.

Nutritional information: calories 152, fat 4g, fibre 3g, carbs 18g, protein 4g

Air Fryer Green Beans

Prep Time: 2 minutes
Cook Time: 8 minutes
Total Time: 10 minutes
Servings: 2

Ingredients:
- 250 g fresh green beans trimmed
- 10 ml olive oil
- 2 g garlic powder (or minced garlic)
- salt and pepper to taste

Preparation:
1. Green beans should be well-washed and dried before cooking. Take the stem off both ends.
2. Place the beans in a basin. Add a few drops of olive oil. To taste, season with salt, pepper, and garlic powder. Mix well until evenly coated.
3. Preheat the air fryer to 200° C. Spread out the seasoned green beans in a single layer

in the air fryer basket (cook in batches if required).
4. At a temperature of 200° C, air-fry them for 7-8 minutes or until tender-crisp. Shake the basket at the halfway mark. Mine were perfectly cooked at 8 minutes.
5. The green beans have been nicely roasted and are now ready. Set it aside, drizzle it with lime juice, and serve immediately.

Nutritional information:
Calories 64 kcal Carbs 8g Protein 2g Fat 3g Fiber 3g Sugar 4g

Air Fryer Roasted Mushrooms

Prep Time 10 minutes
Cook Time 10 minutes
Total Time 20 minutes
Servings 2

Ingredients:
- 250 g Bella mushroom cut into half
- 15 ml olive oil
- 2 g garlic powder (or minced garlic)
- 5 ml soy sauce (or Worcestershire sauce)
- salt and pepper to taste

Garnish
- few lemon wedges
- 15 ml fresh parsley chopped

Preparation:
1. First, clean the mushrooms. Wipe away the grime with a damp kitchen (or paper) towel. Avoid getting wet or going swimming. Cut the mushrooms in half.
2. Combine the mushrooms, soy sauce, olive oil, salt, and pepper with the garlic powder (or minced garlic).
3. Set the temperature of the air fryer to 200° C. In the air fryer basket, arrange the seasoned mushrooms in a single layer (cook in batches if required).
4. Air fry them for 8-10 minutes at 200° C or until golden, juicy, and tender. Shake the basket at the halfway mark.
5. The mushrooms for the air fryer have been prepared. Serve warm after removing from the oven, garnished with lemon juice and freshly chopped parsley.

Nutritional information
Calories 92 Carbohydrates 6g Protein 3g Fat 7g Fiber 1g Sugar 2g

Air Fryer Grilled Panzanella Salad

Prep Time 10 minutes
Cook Time 5 minutes
Total Time 15 minutes
Servings: 2

Ingredients:
- 1 Baguette
- 30 ml olive oil
- 5 g salt
- 2 g black pepper
- 1 English or Persian Cucumber
- 15 ml red wine vinegar
- 60 g pitted olives
- 250 g grape tomatoes
- 30 g diced red onions

- 5 g minced garlic

Preparation:
1. First, make the bread croutons. Season the baguette with salt, pepper, and olive oil after slicing it in half. Place the bread in the air fryer and cook for 4-5 minutes at 180° C. Just enough time to toast the bread.
2. While the bread is toasting, make the vinaigrette by mixing the olive oil, red wine vinegar, minced garlic, salt, and black pepper.
3. After the bread has completed baking, allow it to cool before slicing it. Each piece should be about one inch long.
4. Cut the cucumber in half, the red onions in half, the olives in half, and the tomatoes in half. In a large mixing bowl, combine the tomatoes, olives, red onions, and bread slices. After that, drizzle on the homemade vinegar.
5. Enjoy! Serve immediately!

Nutritional information:
Calories 626 Fat 15g carbohydrates 95 fibre 6g sugar 13g protein 20g

SNACKS AND APPETIZERS

Air Fryer Yorkshire Puddings

Prep Time: 5 mins
Cook Time: 15 mins
Resting time: 30 mins
Total Time: 50 mins
Servings: 12

Ingredients:
For the batter
- 150 g flour, plain / all-purpose flour
- 3 g salt
- 3 large eggs
- 250 ml milk, semi-skimmed

To cook:
- 50 ml vegetable cooking fat (such as Trex) or sunflower oil, as needed

Preparation:
1. Fill a mixing basin halfway with flour. Stir in a sprinkle of salt to mix. Crack the eggs into the bowl, add a splash of milk, and whisk together with a balloon whisk.
2. Mix in the remaining milk gradually until you have a smooth batter. Rest the batter in your refrigerator for 30 mins or overnight.
3. Note: If you have an immersion blender, combine all ingredients in a tall measuring jug and blitz until smooth.
1. Place a silicone muffin pan in the air fryer basket (or ramekins / cake tins). Add 3 ml of vegetable baking fat (or sunflower oil) to each. Preheat the air fryer for 10 minutes at 200°C.
2. Before creating the puddings, thoroughly combine the batter. Working rapidly, pour the batter into the tin, filling it slightly under halfway. Air fried for 10 minutes, or until the puddings are brown and puffy on top but still a little doughy on the bottom.
3. Cook for another 5 minutes for little puddings and up to 10 minutes for bigger ones, using tongs to flip them over. The puddings should have crisp edges and be golden, puffy, and light as air. You may cook them for a bit longer if they are still heavy.
4. Serve with roast meat (or any roast dish) and plenty of gravy!

Nutrition information:
Calories 98 Carbs 9g Protein 3g Fat 5g Cholesterol 43mg Fiber 0.3g Sugar 1g

Mini Sausage Rolls

Prep time: 5 minutes
Cook time: 15 minutes
Servings: 4

Ingredients:
- 1 packet of rolls (flatbread)
- 10 mini beef sausage

Preparation:
1. Cut the rolls into triangles. Each sausage should be wrapped in a rolls triangle until entirely coated.
2. Preheat your air fryer to 180°C and place the rolls in the basket. Bake for 15 minutes, flipping halfway through, or until the rolls are crisp.

Nutritional information:
Carbs. 24 g. Dietary Fiber. 2.6 g. Sugar. 0 g. Fat. 15.4 g. Protein 6.7g

Puff Pastry Banana Rolls

Prep time: 10 minutes
Cook time: 10 minutes
Servings: 3

Ingredients:
- 2 puff pastry sheets
- 3 medium-sized bananas, peeled

Preparation:
1. Cut the pastry sheets into thin strips. Twine two strips together to produce a cord. Make as many cables as needed.
2. Wrap the cords around the bananas until they are completely coated with pastry.
3. Cook the wrapped bananas in the air fryer for 10 minutes, or until golden.

Nutritional information:
Carbs. 55 g Fiber. 9 g Sugar. 23 g Fat. 7 g Saturated. 3 g. Protein 27

Banana Snack

Prep time: 10 minutes
Cook time: 5 minutes
Servings: 8

Ingredients:
- 16 baking cups crust
- 60 g peanut butter
- 120 g chocolate chips
- 1 banana, peeled and sliced into 16 pieces
- 15 ml vegetable oil

Preparation:
1. Put the chocolate chips in a small pot, heat over low heat, stir until melted, and remove from the flame.
2. Whisk together peanut butter and coconut oil in a mixing basin.
3. Fill a cup with 5 g chocolate mix, 1 banana slice, and 5 g butter.
4. Repeat with the remaining cups, then arrange them in a dish that fits your air fryer, cook at 160° C for 5 minutes, transfer to a freezer, and store frozen until ready to serve as a snack.

Nutritional information:
calories 70, fat 4g, fiber 1g, carbs 10g, protein 1g

Pizza Rolls

Prep Time: 15 minutes

Cook Time: 10 minutes
Servings: 24 rolls (3 per serving)

Ingredients:
- 250 g shredded mozzarella cheese
- 50 g almond flour
- 2 large eggs
- 70 slices pepperoni
- 8 (30 g) mozzarella string cheese sticks, cut into 3 pieces each
- 30 g unsalted butter, melted
- 1.5 g garlic powder
- 2.5 g dried Parsley
- 15 g grated Parmesan cheese

Preparation:
1. In a microwave-safe mixing bowl, combine the mozzarella and almond flour. Microwave for 1 minute. Remove the bowl and keep mixing until a ball of dough forms. Microwave for additional 30 seconds if necessary.
2. In the mixing bowl, crack the eggs and whisk until a smooth dough ball forms. Knead the dough for a few seconds with wet hands.
3. Spray two substantial sheets of parchment paper with nonstick cooking spray on one side. Spray the sides of the dough ball and place it between the two sheets. With a rolling pin, roll out the dough to 6 mm thickness.
4. Using a knife, cut the pie into 24 rectangles. Place 3 pepperoni slices and 1 string cheese slice on each rectangle.
5. Fold the rectangle in half to cover the pepperoni and cheese mixture. Close the sides by pinching or rolling them close. Set out a piece of parchment paper the size of your air fryer basket. Arrange the rolls on parchment paper.
6. Set the air fryer to 180°C and the timer to 10 minutes.
7. Remove the pizza rolls from the fryer and flip them after 5 minutes. Re-heat the frying until the pizza rolls are browned.
8. In a medium bowl, combine the butter, garlic powder, and parsley. Brush the mixture on the cooked pizza rolls and sprinkle with Parmesan. Serve immediately.

Nutritional information:
calories: 333 protein: 20.7 g fiber: 0.8 g fat: 24.0 g Carbohydrates: 3.3 g Sugar: 0.9 g

Courgette Cakes

Prep time: 10 minutes
Cook time: 12 minutes
Servings: 12

Ingredients:
- Cooking spray
- 70 g dill, chopped
- 1 egg
- 70 g wholemeal flour
- Salt and black pepper to the taste
- 1 yellow onion, chopped
- 2 garlic cloves, minced
- 3 courgette, grated

Preparation:
1. Whisk together the courgette, garlic, onion, flour, salt, pepper, egg, and dill in a mixing basin. Form small patties from this mixture, coat with cooking spray, and cook for 6 minutes on each side at 190° C.

2. Serve them as a snack right away.

Nutritional information:
calories 60, fat 1g, fiber 2g, carbs 6g, protein 2g

Banana Chips

Prep time: 10 minutes
Cook time: 15 minutes
Servings: 4

Ingredients:
- 4 bananas, peeled and sliced
- A pinch of salt
- 2 g turmeric powder
- 2.5 g chat masala
- 10 ml olive oil

Preparation:
1. In a mixing bowl, toss banana slices with salt, turmeric, chat masala, and oil for 10 minutes.
2. Cook the banana slices in your preheated air fryer for 15 minutes, turning once.
3. Serve as a snack.

Nutritional information:
calories 121, fat 1g, fiber 2g, carbs 3g, protein 3g

Chickpeas Snack

Prep time: 10 minutes
Cook time: 10 minutes
Servings: 4

Ingredients:
- 400 g canned chickpeas, drained
- 2.5 g cumin, ground
- 20 ml olive oil
- 5 g smoked paprika
- Salt and black pepper to the taste

Preparation:
1. Toss chickpeas in a bowl with oil, cumin, paprika, salt, and pepper to cover, then place in a fryer basket and cook for 10 minutes at 210° C.
2. Serve in separate bowls as a snack.

Nutritional information:
calories 140, fat 1g, fiber 6g, carbs 20g, protein 6g

Egg White Chips

Prep time: 5 minutes
Cook time: 8 minutes
Servings: 2

Ingredients:
- 10 ml water
- 15 g parmesan, shredded
- 4 eggs whites

- Salt and black pepper to the taste

Preparation:
1. Mix egg whites, salt, pepper, and water in a mixing bowl.
2. Spoon into an air fryer-compatible muffin tray, cover with cheese, and bake at 180 degrees Celsius for 8 minutes.
3. Serve the egg white chips on a dish as a snack.

Nutritional information:
calories 180, fat 2g, fiber 1g, carbs 12g, protein 7g

Pesto Crackers

Prep time: 10 minutes
Cook time: 17 minutes
Servings: 6

Ingredients:
- 3 g bicarbonate of soda
- Salt and black pepper to the taste
- 200 g flour
- 2 g basil, dried
- 1 garlic clove, minced
- 30 g basil pesto
- 40 g butter

Preparation:
1. In a mixing bowl, combine salt, pepper, bicarbonate of soda, flour, garlic, cayenne pepper, basil, pesto, and butter until a dough forms.
2. Bake for 17 minutes at 170 degrees Celsius on a prepared baking sheet that fits your air fryer.
3. Allow it cool completely before slicing into crackers and serving as a snack.

Nutritional information:
Calories 200, fat 20, fibre 1, carbs 4, protein 7

Roasted Garlic

Prep time 5 minutes
Cook Time: 20 minutes
Serving: 12 cloves (1 per serving)

Ingredients
- 1 medium head garlic
- 10 ml avocado oil

Preparation:
1. Remove the garlic skin but leave the cloves alone. Remove 1/4 of the garlic head, exposing the clove tips.
2. To finish, drizzle with avocado oil. Wrap the garlic head completely in a thin layer of aluminium foil. Fill half of the air fryer basket with it.
3. Set the air fryer to 210°C set the timer to 20 minutes. If your garlic head is smaller, check it after 15 minutes.
4. The garlic should be golden brown and extremely tender when done.
5. The cloves should easily be dispersed or chopped when ready to serve. Refrigerate for 5 days in an airtight container. Individual cloves can also be frozen on a baking sheet before being placed in a freezer-safe storage bag.

Nutritional information:
Calories: 11 Protein 0.3 g Fiber 0.1 g Fat 0.8 g Carbs 1.1 g

Stuffed Peppers

Prep time: 10 minutes
Cook time: 8 minutes
Servings: 8

Ingredients:
- 8 small red peppers, tops cut off and seeds removed
- 15 ml olive oil
- Salt and black pepper to the taste
- 100 g goat cheese, cut into 8 pieces

Preparation:
1. Mix the cheese, oil, salt, and pepper in a mixing dish.
2. Stuff each pepper with goat cheese and cook for 8 minutes at 220° C in an air fryer basket. Place on a plate and serve as an appetizer.

Nutritional information:
calories 120, fat 1g, fiber 1g, carbs 12g, protein 8g

Avocado Fries

Prep Time: 15 minutes
Cook Time: 5 minutes
Serving: 4

Ingredients:
- 2 medium avocados
- 30 g pork rinds, finely ground

Preparation:
1. Each avocado is cut in half. Remove the pit. After carefully detaching the flesh, cut it into 14" thick slices.
2. Place the pork rinds in a medium bowl and press each avocado slice into the pork rinds to coat equally. Place the avocado slices in the air fryer basket.
3. Set the timer for 5 minutes and heat the water to 185°C.
4. Serve immediately.

Nutritional information:
calories 153 protein 5.4 g fibre 4.6 g fat 11.7 g Carbs 5.9 g

Air Fryer Frozen Okra

Prep Time 0 mins
Cook Time 15 mins
Servings: 3

Ingredients:
- 500 g frozen okra
- olive oil spray or 5 ml olive oil
- 2 g garlic
- 2 g black pepper
- 2.5 g salt
- Red pepper flakes optional, garnish

Preparation:
1. Preheat your air fryer to 210 degrees Celsius.
2. Arrange the frozen okra in a single layer in the air fryer basket.
3. Cooking spray should be used to coat the okra.
4. Combine the spices in a small dish and sprinkle over the frozen okra.
5. Shake the basket or use a brush to gently rub the spices all over.
6. After 15 minutes of air cooking, shake the basket.
7. Garnish with red pepper flakes and serve!

Nutritional information:
Calories 33kcal Carbs 7g Protein 1g Fat 1g Fiber 4g Sugar 1g

Herbed Tomatoes Appetizer

Prep time: 10 minutes
Cook time: 20 minutes
Servings: 2

Ingredients:
- 2 tomatoes, halved
- Cooking spray
- Salt and black pepper to the taste
- 5 g parsley, dried
- 5 g basil, dried
- 5 g oregano, dried
- 5 g rosemary, dried

Preparation:
1. Spray tomato halves with cooking oil before seasoning with salt, pepper, parsley, basil, oregano, and rosemary.
2. Cook for 20 minutes at 170° C in an air fryer basket.
3. Arrange them on a platter to serve as an appetiser.

Nutritional information:
calories 100, fat 1g, fiber 1g, carbs 4g, protein 1g

Roasted Pepper Rolls

Prep time: 10 minutes
Cook time: 10 minutes
Servings: 8

Ingredients:
- 1 yellow pepper, halved
- 1 orange pepper, halved
- Salt and black pepper to the taste
- 120 g feta cheese, crumbled
- 1 green onion, chopped
- 5 g oregano, chopped

Preparation:
1. Mix the cheese, onion, oregano, salt, and pepper in a mixing bowl.
2. Cook for 10 minutes in the air fryer basket at 210° C, then transfer to a chopping board to cool and peel.
3. Roll each pepper half in the cheese mixture, secure with toothpicks, and serve as an appetiser.

Nutritional information:
calories 170, fat 1g, fiber 2g, carbs 8g, protein 5g

Salmon Party Patties

Prep time: 10 minutes
Cook time: 22 minutes
Servings: 4

Ingredients:
- 3 big potatoes, boiled, drained, and mashed
- 1 big salmon fillet, skinless, boneless
- 8 g parsley, chopped
- 7 g dill, chopped
- Salt and black pepper to the taste
- 1 egg
- 15 g bread crumbs
- Cooking spray

Preparation:
1. Cook the fish for 10 minutes at 190° Celsius in the air fryer basket.
2. Allow the salmon to cool on a cutting board before flaking it into a bowl.

3. Mix in the mashed potatoes, salt, pepper, dill, parsley, egg, and bread crumbs, and shape the mixture into 8 patties.
4. Place the salmon patties in the air fryer basket, spray with cooking oil, and cook for 12 minutes, flipping halfway. Transfer to a serving platter and serve as an appetizer.

Nutritional information:
calories 231, fat 3, fiber 7, carbs 14, protein 4

Kale Chips

Prep Time: 5 minutes
Cook Time: 5 minutes
Serving: 4

Ingredients:
- 4 cups stemmed kale
- 10 ml avocado oil
- 3 g salt

Preparation:
1. Combine kale, avocado oil, and salt in a large mixing bowl. Place in your air fryer basket.
2. Set the thermostat to 205° C and a timer for 5 minutes.
3. Kale will be crisp when cooked. Serve immediately.

Nutritional information: calories: 25 protein: 0.6 g fiber: 0.4 g fat: 2.1 g Carbos: 1.1 g

Spinach Balls

Prep time: 10 minutes
Cook time: 7 minutes
Servings: 30

Ingredients:
- 50 g butter, melted
- 2 eggs
- 250 g flour
- 450 g spinach
- 50 g feta cheese, crumbled
- 1.2 g nutmeg, ground
- 30 g parmesan, grated
- Salt and black pepper to the taste
- 15 g onion powder
- 15 g double cream
- 5 g garlic powder

Preparation:
1. In a blender, combine the spinach, butter, eggs, flour, feta cheese, parmesan, nutmeg, double cream, salt, pepper, onion, and garlic until smooth. Place for 10 minutes in the freezer.
2. Form 30 spinach balls, place them in the air fryer basket, and cook for 7 mins at 160° C.
3. During a party, serve as an appetiser.

Nutritional information:
calories 60, fat 5g, fiber 1g, carbs 1g, protein 2g

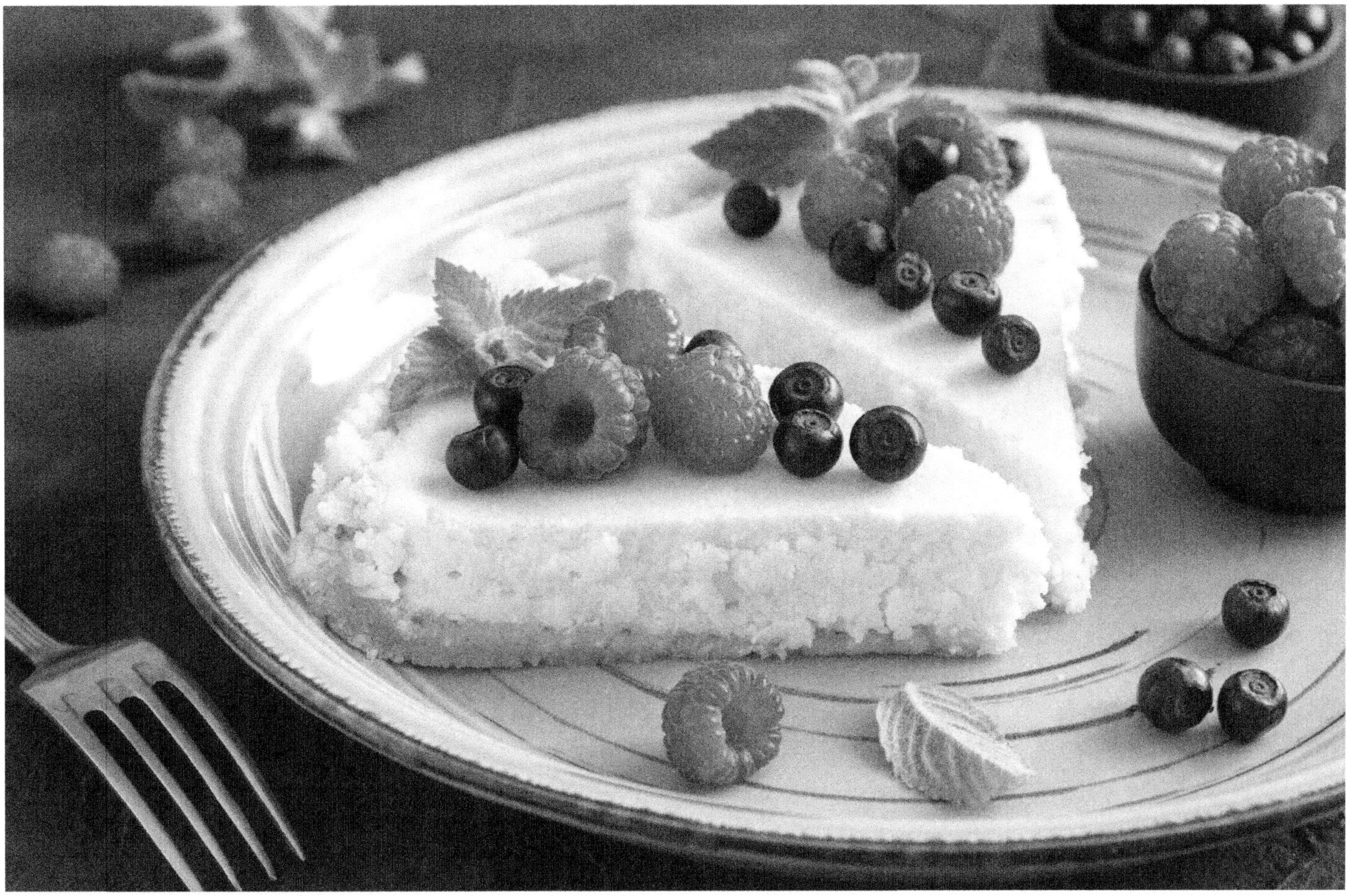

DESSERTS

Air Fryer Scones Recipe

Prep time: 15 minutes
Cook time: 15 minutes
Total time: 30 minutes
Servings: 6

Ingredients:
- 450 g self-rising flour
- 80 g unsalted butter, chilled and cubed
- 250 ml milk

To Serve
- Raspberry Jam
- Whipped Cream

Preparation:
1. Preheat the air fryer to 160 degrees Celsius. It will take around 5 minutes to heat up.
2. Combine the chilled butter and flour in a large mixing basin. The butter should be rubbed into the flour until it resembles bread crumbs.
3. Create a well in the centre of the flour. Add the milk to the centre and combine with a flat-bladed knife until smooth. The dough should be pliable; if it is too dry, gradually add additional milk.
4. Knead the dough on a lightly floured board until smooth. Excessive kneading will result in tough scones.
5. Roll out the dough to a thickness of about 2 cm. Cut out as many pieces as you can with a 5cm circular scone cutter. Combine the dough and cut out the leftover pieces. If necessary, repeat.
6. Fill the bottom of the air fryer basket with baking paper. Place the scones so that they are virtually touching on the paper. You'll probably have to cook in batches.
7. Cook the scones for 15 minutes or until golden brown and sound hollow when tapped.
8. Serve immediately and enjoy.

Nutrition Information:
Calories 388 Fat 13g Carbs 58g Fiber 2g Sugars 2g Cholesterol 33mg Protein 9g

Pan Peanut Butter Cookies

Prep Time: 5 minutes
Cook Time: 8 minutes
Serving: 8

Ingredients:
- 250 g no-sugar-added smooth peanut butter
- 8 g granular erythritol
- 1 large egg
- 5 ml vanilla extract

Preparation:
1. In a medium mixing bowl, combine all the ingredients. After two minutes of churning, the liquid will begin to thicken.
2. Form eight discs of the mixture by rolling it into balls and gently pressing down.
3. Cut a piece of parchment to size and place it in the basket of your air fryer. Working in batches, arrange the cookies on parchment paper.
4. Set the timer for 8 minutes and change the temperature to 160°C.

5. Turn the cookies after six minutes. Serve once completely chilled.

Nutritional information:
calories 210 protein 8.8 g fiber 2.0 g fat 17.5 g Carbohydrates 14.1 g Sugar 1.1 g

Raspberry Danish Bites

Prep Time: 30 mins
Cook Time: 7 mins
Servings: 10

Ingredients:
- 100 g blanched finely ground almond flour
- 5 g bicarbonate of soda
- 50 g granular Swerve
- 60 g full-fat cream cheese, softened
- 1 large egg
- 150 g sugar-free raspberry preserves

Preparation:
1. In a large mixing basin, combine all ingredients except the preserves until a wet dough forms.
2. Freeze the bowl for 20 minutes or until the dough is cold enough to form into a ball.
3. Roll the dough into ten balls, then press each one gently in the centre. Each ball should have 15 g of preserves in the centre.
4. Line your air fryer basket with parchment paper.

5. Place each Danish bite on the parchment paper, carefully flattening the bottom.
6. Set the temperature of your air fryer to 205°C and the timer to 7 minutes.
7. To avoid collapse, allow it to cool completely before transferring.

Nutritional information:
Calories 96 Protein 3 g fibre 1.3 g fat 8 g Carbohydrates 10 g Sugar: 2 g

Mini Cheesecake

Prep Time: 10 mins
Cook Time: 15 mins
Servings: 2

Ingredients:
- 50 g walnuts
- 30 g salted butter
- 30 ml granular erythritol
- 100 g full-fat cream cheese, softened
- 1 large egg
- 2.5 ml vanilla extract
- 30 g powdered erythritol

Preparation:
1. In a food processor, combine walnuts, butter, and granular erythritol. Pulse the ingredients until a dough forms.
2. In a 10 cm springform pan, place the dough in the air fryer basket.

3. Set the temperature of the air fryer to 210° C and the timer to 5 minutes.
4. When the timer goes off, take the crust from the oven, and set it aside to cool.
5. Blend the cream cheese, egg, vanilla extract, and powdered erythritol in a medium mixing bowl until smooth.
6. Place the air fryer basket in the air fryer and spoon the ingredients on top of the cooked walnut crust.
7. Set the temperature of your air fryer to 150° C and the timer to 10 minutes.
8. Allow at least two hours before serving to chill.

Nutritional information:
Calories 531 Protein 11 g fibre 2.3 g fat 48.3 g Carbs 31 g Sugar 3 g

Calories 165 protein 1 g fibre 3 g fat: 15 g carbs 20 g sugar 0.5 g

Pecan Brownies

Prep Time: 10 minutes
Cook Time: 20 minutes
Servings: 6

Ingredients:
- 50 g blanched finely ground almond flour
- 100 g powdered erythritol
- 30 g unsweetened cocoa powder
- 3 g bicarbonate of soda
- 60 g unsalted butter, softened
- 1 large egg
- 30 g chopped pecans
- 40 g low-carb, sugar-free chocolate chips

Preparation:
1. Combine almond flour, erythritol, cocoa powder, and Bicarbonate of soda in a large mixing bowl. Mix in the butter and egg.
2. In a mixing dish, combine the pecans and chocolate chips. Halfway fill a 15 cm circular baking pan with the ingredients. Insert the pan into the air fryer basket.
3. Set the temperature of the air fryer to 160°C and the timer to 20 minutes.
4. A toothpick put into the centre should come out clean when fully cooked. Allow 20 minutes for the mixture to cool and firm up.

Toasted Coconut Flakes

Prep Time: 5 mins
Cook Time: 3 mins
Servings: 4

Ingredients:
- 100 g unsweetened coconut flakes
- 10 ml coconut oil
- 60 g granular erythritol
- 1 g salt

Preparation:
1. In a large mixing basin, toss the coconut flakes with the oil until uniformly covered. Season with salt and erythritol to taste.
2. Coconut flakes should cover half of the air fryer basket.
3. Set the temperature of the air fryer to 160°C and the timer to 3 minutes.
4. Throw the flakes after one minute. Cook for another minute if you like a more golden coconut flake.
5. Store in an airtight container for up to three days.

Nutritional information:

Nutritional information:
Calories 215 Protein 4 g fibre: 3 g fat 19 g Carbs 22 g Sugar 1 g

Crispy Apple

Prep time: 10 minutes
Cook time: 10 minutes
Servings: 4

Ingredients:
- 10 ml cassia
- 5 apples, cored and cut into chunks
- 2 g nutmeg powder
- 15 ml golden syrup
- 120 ml water
- 60 g butter
- 40 g flour
- 70 g old-fashioned rolled oats
- 50 g light brown sugar

Preparation:
1. Place the apples, cassia nutmeg, golden syrup, and water in an air fryer-safe pan.
2. Whisk together the butter, oats, sugar, salt, and flour. Drop spoonful of this mixture on top of the apples; place in the air fryer and cook for 10 minutes at 180° C.
3. Serve immediately.

Nutritional information: calories 200, fat 6, fibre 8, carbs 29, protein 12

Strawberry Pie

Prep time: 10 minutes
Cook time: 20 minutes
Servings: 12

Ingredients:
For the crust:
- 100 g coconut, shredded
- 130 g sunflower seeds
- 60 g butter

For the filling:
- 5 ml gelatin
- 250 g cream cheese
- 120 g strawberries
- 30 ml water
- 7.5 ml lemon juice
- 1.2 g stevia
- 120 ml double cream
- 200 g strawberries, chopped for serving

Preparation:
1. Combine sunflower seeds, coconut, a pinch of salt, and butter in a food processor, pulse, and press into the bottom of an air fryer cake pan.
2. In a saucepan over medium heat, heat the water, then add the gelatin and stir until dissolved. Allow cooling before mixing in a food processor with the 120 g

strawberries, cream cheese, lemon juice, and stevia.
3. Stir in the double cream and spread it evenly over the crust.
4. Top with 200 g strawberries and cook for 15 minutes at 170° C in an air fryer.
5. Place in the refrigerator until ready to serve.

Nutritional information:
Calories 234, fat 23, fibre 2 g, carbs 6 g, protein 7 g

Bread Dough and Amaretto Dessert

Prep time: 10 minutes
Cook time: 12 minutes
Servings: 12

Ingredients:
- 500 g bread dough
- 200 g sugar
- 100 g butter, melted
- 250 ml double cream
- 350 g chocolate chips
- 30 ml amaretto liqueur

Preparation:
1. Roll out the dough and cut it into 20 pieces, then halve each slice.
2. Brush the dough pieces with butter, sprinkle with sugar, and place them in the air fryer basket after brushing with butter. Cook for 5 minutes at 180° C, turn them and cook for 3 minutes further before transferring them to a dish.
3. In a saucepan over medium heat, heat the double cream, then add the chocolate chips and stir until they melt.
4. Transfer to a bowl and serve with bread dippers after stirring in the liquor.

Nutritional information:
Calories 200, fat 1, fibre 0, carbs 6, protein 6

Chocolate Cookies

Prep time: 10 minutes
Cook time: 25 minutes
Servings: 12

Ingredients:
- 5 ml vanilla extract
- 100 g butter
- 1 egg
- 50 g sugar
- 250 g flour
- 100 g unsweetened chocolate chips

Preparation:
1. In a pan over medium heat, melt the butter, stir, and cook for 1 minute.
2. In a mixing bowl, thoroughly combine the egg, vanilla extract, and sugar.
3. Combine the melted butter, flour, and half of the chocolate chips in a mixing bowl.
4. Transfer to an air fryer-safe pan, top with the remaining chocolate chips, and bake for 25 minutes at 175° C.
5. Serve when it's cold enough to slice.

Nutritional information:
Calories 230, fat 12g, fibre 2g, carbs 4g, protein 5g

Mini Lava Cakes

Prep time: 10 minutes
Cook time: 20 minutes
Servings: 3

Ingredients:
- 1 egg
- 50 g sugar
- 30 ml olive oil
- 60 ml milk
- 30 g flour
- 7 g cocoa powder
- 2.5 g Bicarbonate of soda
- 2.5 g orange zest

Preparation:
1. Combine the egg, sugar, oil, milk, flour, salt, cocoa powder, Bicarbonate of soda, and orange zest in a mixing bowl; whisk well and pour into prepared ramekins.
2. Cook the ramekins for 20 minutes at 170° C in the air fryer.
3. Lava cakes should be served warmly.

Nutritional information:
Calories 201, fat 7 g, fibre 8 g, carbs 23 g, protein 4 g

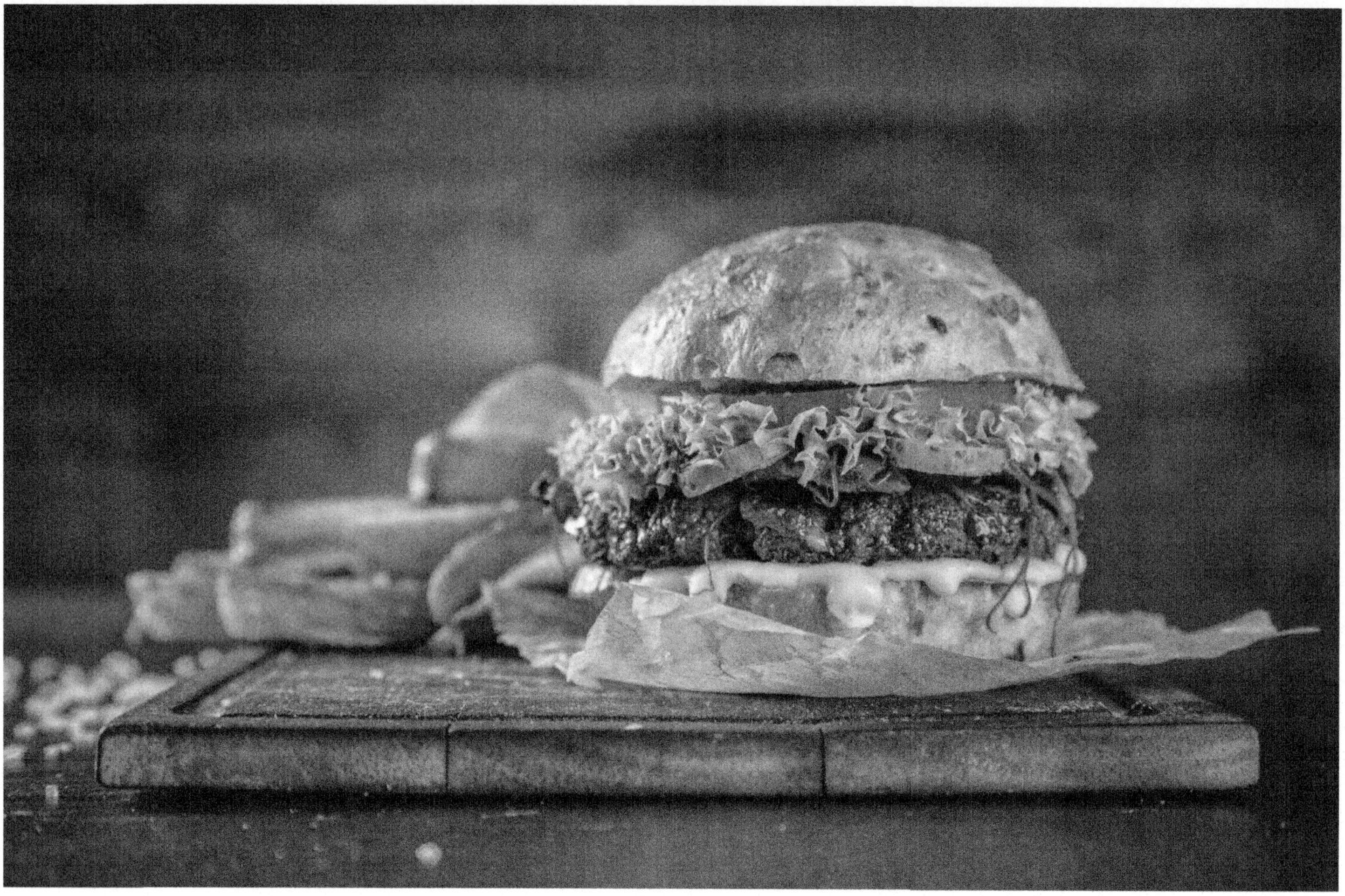

Printed in Great Britain
by Amazon